Classroom Talk

Evidence-based Teaching
for Enquiring Teachers

Classroom Talk

Evidence-based Teaching
for Enquiring Teachers

Rupert Knight

Routledge
Taylor & Francis Group

LONDON AND NEW YORK

First published in 2020 by Critical Publishing Ltd

Published 2025 by Routledge
4 Park Square, Milton Park, Abingdon, Oxon OX14 4RN
605 Third Avenue, New York, NY 10017

Routledge is an imprint of the Taylor & Francis Group, an informa business

British Library Cataloguing in Publication Data

A CIP record for this book is available from the British Library

ISBN: 9781912508853 (pbk)
ISBN: 9781041054511 (ebk)

Cover design by Out of House Limited
Text design by Out of House Limited

DOI: 10.4324/9781041054511

Acknowledgements

I would like to thank Julia Morris, from Critical Publishing, and Val Poultney, as series editor, for their prompt and encouraging feedback at all stages in the writing of this book. My thanks also go to the many schools, colleagues and pupils I have worked with in education over the years who have provided the inspiration for the examples in the chapters that follow.

Rupert Knight

Contents

Meet the series editor and author

Val Poultney

Val Poultney is a senior lecturer at the University of Derby. She teaches on initial teacher education and postgraduate programmes. Her research interests include school leadership and school governance with a particular focus on how to develop leadership to support teachers as researchers.

Rupert Knight

Rupert Knight was a school teacher in London and Nottingham before moving into higher education. He is now Assistant Professor at the University of Nottingham, working with student and practising teachers in England and overseas. His research interests include the relationship between theory and practice in learning to teach.

Foreword

Our education system is arguably one of the most complex in the world and ever evolving. Teaching professionals face competing demands on a daily basis as they strive to maintain high standards of teaching and learning in a system which is in a constant state of flux. However, among such complexity there has been one enduring theme of the 'self-improving school', and at grass-roots classroom level it is teachers who bear the weight of constantly looking for ways to improve pupil learning. We have, so far in this series, argued that in order to improve outcomes for pupils, educators should be critically engaging with research as both consumers and producers to provide them with the evidence to reflect on their practice.

In this latest addition to the series *Evidence-based Teaching for Enquiring Teachers* Rupert Knight examines issues around classroom talk. Rupert is an assistant professor at the University of Nottingham and has a special interest in classroom talk and collaboration. He argues that classroom dialogue is a powerful medium through which both pupil and teacher learning can take place. What is arguably a taken-for-granted activity between teachers and their pupils is in fact a far more complex interaction than we might imagine. Through a series of questions around three distinct areas of classroom dialogue, Rupert encourages us to consider the social, cultural and political dimensions of how we use our spoken language in classrooms. He goes on to examine in detail how pupils receive and construct knowledge, the effect of language on relationships between teachers and their pupils, and the different types of language most commonly used in schools.

The importance of oracy in education is now a re-emerging theme, which brings to the fore a whole body of academic research and publication in this field. This is highlighted by the Oracy All Party Parliamentary Group (Oracy APPG, 2019) who have raised concerns about the importance of oracy in state education. The view is that spoken language use in schools is currently undervalued and potentially underdeveloped. In response an inquiry was set up to examine the quality of this provision. Alongside quality issues the inquiry investigated the value of oracy in terms of development of language skills to enhance pupil achievement, social mobility, well-being and employability, and any potential barriers to accessing oracy education.

In these times of change it is important for educators to have access to a range of evidence which can inform and direct practice. Furthermore, this evidence should be easily accessible to a range of educators: teacher professionals, trainee teachers, school mentors and university academics as well as educators more widely. Rupert's book provides a highly readable and informative introduction to classroom talk, providing links to academic research and school case studies that encourage teachers to reflect on their own approach to classroom talk and how important dialogue is for learning. This, during a period of emerging government interest in this area of education, makes Rupert's book a very timely publication.

Val Poultney, series editor
Senior lecturer in Education, University of Derby

Reference

Oracy All Party Parliamentary Group (2019) *Speak for Change (new enquiry).* [online] Available at: www.oracyappg.org.uk (accessed 18 July 2019).

Chapter 1
Introducing and mapping debates around classroom talk

1.1 Chapter overview

This chapter will outline:

1.2   what is meant by classroom talk and the scope of the book;

1.3   why an evidence-informed approach is important;

1.4   how you can make sense of research in this field;

1.5   key debates and questions to be explored.

1.2 Introduction: what is meant by classroom talk and what is the scope of this book?

Take a walk along a school corridor, pause outside a classroom door and listen. There are voices, but whose voices? What are they saying and why? Perhaps a teacher is introducing a new concept to a class and asking questions to check understanding or provoke new thinking. Perhaps the voice heard is not the teacher's at all, but that of a pupil answering or asking a question. Perhaps pupils are talking to one another independently of the teacher. Sometimes there is consensus, sometimes debate and disagreement. Tuning in and trying to discern the meaning and dynamics of this complex mixture of spoken language might give rise to a number of questions.

A first set relates to participation and the learner's role in this process. Are pupils passive recipients of knowledge, or active participants in the construction of understanding? The stance taken on this determines particular classroom routines and consequently patterns of spoken interaction. A second set of questions concerns the purpose and content of this interaction. To what extent is learning predetermined by the teacher, with pupils guided along a set path? To what extent, in contrast, are pupils invited to engage in open, authentic dialogue? Is talk between pupils purely social and a distraction from learning, or can peer talk be productive for learning? Finally, questions might be raised about the form of spoken language employed in all of these scenarios. Are there modes of speech that are more cognitively or socially desirable than others and, if so, should talk be an object of learning in its own right? Some positions taken by teachers on these questions may be strongly value-related and embedded in the purposes of education more widely. From this starting point, the aim of this book is to consider the evidence around what is known – and not known – about classroom talk.

Moving beyond the mere ubiquity of talk in classrooms, it is important to question why it is particularly worthy of your attention. After all, while spoken language is the medium through which much teaching and learning takes place, its purposes and conventions are often very different from talk in everyday life. There are three broad arguments, each with its own strand of research, that have been made for a focus on classroom talk.

1. The psychological or cognitive argument: the idea that learning and development are shaped heavily – though not exclusively – by social interaction. For example, Mercer and Littleton (2007) explain that cognitive development and learning are mediated by cultural and social activities such as talk and that learning can be thought of as the joint construction of understanding through a process of dialogue.

2. The sociological argument: an interest in principles such as identity, inclusion and communicative rights, whereby authentic pupil voice and ownership of learning have a place in classrooms. For example, Lefstein and Snell (2014) provide a critique of typical classroom discourse structures in terms of their promotion of a narrow, uncritical acceptance of knowledge and authority.

3. The communicative competence argument: the idea that capability with spoken language is an essential skill for success in education and beyond. For example, Bruner (1978) notes that such competence goes beyond a grasp of syntax and semantics and depends on the sophisticated social use of dialogue. For some, this includes valuing the richness of informal language, while for others this has been about the use of 'correct' standard forms.

In this book, therefore, you will be able to evaluate arguments for classroom talk not only on the basis of pedagogy and academic achievement, but also in light of cultural, social and political considerations. The case for talk is neatly previewed by Alexander's (2012) summing up of the understanding of the role played by high-quality talk in the following:

- contributing to children's development, thinking and learning as a form of pedagogy;

- closing equity gaps due to social disadvantage;

- enhancing employability and social and economic well-being;
- promoting democratic involvement in learning and student voice;
- helping teachers to assess pupils' understanding formatively.

Nevertheless, such arguments are by no means universally accepted or enacted. Within the UK, for example, the effects of what Sahlberg (2016) calls the Global Education Reform Movement have been felt. They include increased standardisation of teaching and a focus on prescribed content transmitted in a risk-averse, often teacher-led, mode. Meanwhile, the national curriculum's (DfE, 2013) spoken language strand within the English curriculum positions talk largely as a skill to underpin reading and writing. This calls to mind Alexander's (2014) vivid report of a government minister's caution, during a curriculum review, about the danger of being seen to *encourage idle chatter in class* (p 357). In order to explore the case for talk rigorously, therefore, a careful review of the evidence base is required.

The scope of this book is primarily the evidence on *promoting the use of high-quality talk by pupils as a means, but also the object, of learning*. This means that some forms of classroom talk necessarily fall outside this boundary, but this is not a reflection of their importance. For example, teacher exposition through explanation and modelling is a central part of any educator's repertoire, but will be discussed only in so far as this relates to more interactive forms of talk. Similarly, the all-important social relationships formed through informal peer talk will be considered largely for their value in promoting academic learning. In this book, then, the focus is on spoken interaction at classroom level, across age phases, as a mode of thinking and communicating and a means of jointly constructing understanding.

1.3 Why is an evidence-informed approach important?

A detailed account of current approaches to, and benefits of, the use of evidence to inform education is provided by Philpott and Poultney (2018) in this series. It is fair to say, however, that the relationship between research and teaching has sometimes been an uneasy one, with claims that there has historically been a mismatch between the knowledge required by teachers and that generated by researchers (Cain, 2015). In recent years, there has been a renewed interest in connecting teachers more directly with evidence. This arises in part from arguments for greater teacher autonomy, linked to a research-literate teaching community, active as both informed *consumers* and *producers* of evidence (BERA, 2014). This argument is strongly associated with the vision of a 'self-improving' school system, championed in England, for example, in government reforms (DfE, 2010). While there is much to admire in this school-led stance, it might also be seen as a product of the shift in some parts of the world towards standardisation, measurement, comparison and competition mentioned in Section 1.2.

Some have also called into question an impoverished, 'what works' view of what constitutes evidence and how it might be used. Biesta (2016), for example, draws attention to the emphasis on effectiveness and argues that this term has little meaning unless it is clear what an action is effective *for*. There are many potential value systems and purposes for education, beyond simply improving attainment, rendering a single response impossible. Others have questioned the privileging of 'scientific' approaches to research, such as randomised control trials (RCTs). Attractive for their promise of an experimental, controlled trial of an intervention, potentially establishing causation, they may not always take into account context and experience. Connolly et al (2018) reflect these concerns and others in their systematic review of RCTs in education, but also conclude that this approach can make an important contribution to understanding if used appropriately. A further issue raised with a simplistic effectiveness view is that it may encourage shortcuts and a superficial use of evidence. Meta-analyses involve an aggregation of outcomes from previous studies and the calculation of an effect size for an intervention. They provide an opportunity to compare and even rank strategies at scale (eg EEF, 2018a; Hattie, 2009) but the feasibility of meaningfully comparing disparate research studies around a broad theme and determining a single effect size has been questioned (Wrigley, 2018).

Rather than view these issues as obstacles, they might instead be seen to suggest three implications for teachers.

1. The need to take an informed and critical stance when presented with research evidence, particularly of the easily digestible, 'what works' variety. Research summaries and meta-analyses, for example, can be very useful tools but the story behind ranked interventions needs to be understood.

2. The importance of going beyond a view of effectiveness as improved attainment to consider the wider purposes of education. This links to the three lines of argument, with their three aims, discussed in Section 1.2.

3. The value of exploring the research around a subject in some depth and achieving a nuanced and reasonably balanced perspective on the topic. This is largely the purpose of this book and indeed this whole series.

1.4 How can you make sense of research in this field?

Navigating the research field

Substantial research interest in classroom talk dates largely from the 1970s. While there are important antecedents, such as the thinking from the 1920s and 1930s of Lev Vygotsky, even this work became widely known only after its translation into English from the 1960s onwards. The interdisciplinary nature of this research field makes it a complex one to navigate and some of the impetus has come from outside education. Early seminal studies, therefore, include those from a linguistic perspective, concerned chiefly with the structure of language use, rather than its meaning (Sinclair and Coulthard, 1975) and those using a more ethnographic approach, exploring context and relationships (Edwards and Furlong, 1978). Since the 1980s, much of the work has coalesced around two key approaches, characterised by Mercer (2010) as *linguistic ethnography* and *sociocultural research*. The linguistic ethnography tradition explores the interaction of language with social and cultural context, while sociocultural researchers focus chiefly on dialogue and collaboration as a tool for learning. From the 1980s onwards, a notable body of work has been the detailed analysis of talk conducted by sociocultural researchers in an attempt to develop analytical frameworks (eg Mercer, 1995). This has led to a degree of consensus around typical forms of naturally occurring classroom talk. Since then, another important focus has become the use of this understanding to articulate and trial more productive models of talk, sometimes in the form of teaching structured repertoires such as collaborative reasoning (eg Clark et al, 2003) and sometimes as broader approaches to pedagogy, such as dialogic teaching (eg Alexander, 2017).

The limitations of research in this field and the possible ways forward are considered more fully in Chapter 7, but it is clear that, within this diverse body of research, there exist certain patterns of emphasis. Howe and Abedin's (2013) systematic review of research on classroom dialogue finds, for example, a field dominated by Western and particularly UK and US research, with the proportion of UK research increasing in recent years. The same review notes a curricular emphasis on science especially, but also mathematics and English. The evidence base is also skewed in its age focus towards primary and early secondary pupils. In discussing the relative lack of research in secondary classrooms, Higham et al (2014) suggest various possible reasons, including the greater capacity in primary education for engaging with new pedagogies in a sustained and holistic way. Finally, Howe and Abedin (2013) note a preponderance of small-scale qualitative research – unsurprising, given the focus on close examination of dialogue. What is beginning to emerge now, however, according to Resnick and Schantz (2015) is a body of experimental studies, more rigorously testing models of classroom talk and starting to provide evidence of transfer to other contexts. The research map which follows attempts to represent some key milestones in this research field chronologically, including some examples of important publications mentioned in this book.

A classroom talk research map and timeline

1960s onwards

Systematic research, usually quantitative and focused on categorising observable features rather than on meaning. Often associated with teacher effectiveness.

* Flanders (1961)

* Galton et al (1980; 1999)

Researching spoken language competence (eg oracy and different 'registers').

* Wilkinson (1965)

* Bernstein (1971)

* Heath (1983)

* Mercer et al (2017a)

1970s onwards

Linguistic research, based on analysis of transcripts to discern language structure and functions.

* Sinclair and Coulthard (1975)

* Mehan (1979)

Sociolinguistic research, based on analysis also focusing on the function and meaning of language.

* Barnes and Todd (1977)

* Edwards and Furlong (1978)

Social constructivist research on learning through scaffolding and contingent teaching.

* Wood et al (1976)

* Bruner (1978)

Ethnographic and sociocultural research with an interest in context and the development of analytic frameworks (eg exploratory talk).

* Edwards and Westgate (1994)

* Mercer (1995)

* Wells (1999)

Researching the impact of productive models of talk (eg exploratory talk; reciprocal teaching; collaborative reasoning; accountable talk).

* Palinscar and Brown (1984)

* Mercer (2000)

* Clark et al (2003)

* Michaels et al (2008)

Dialogic teaching research, with a focus on classroom culture and community to promote effective learning.

* Nystrand et al (2003)

* Mortimer and Scott (2003)

* Alexander (2017)

Experimental research designs and an interest in transfer of learning

* O'Connor et al (2015)

* Sun et al (2015)

* Alexander (2018)

1.5 What are the key debates and questions?

As might be expected from the preceding discussions about the nature of evidence and the diverse, multi-disciplinary perspectives informing the study of talk, this is a complex and contested field. In this section, a dialogue of contrasting views is offered as a way of introducing some of the key debates explored in the chapters that follow. On the left are justifications for classroom talk and on the right are possible counter-arguments.

Arguments around talk in the classroom

> Learning is a social activity, mediated through talk, so we need to give spoken language and social interaction a higher status within the classroom.

(Bruner, 1978; Vygotsky, 1978)

> But acknowledging this social constructivist view of learning doesn't necessarily imply any particular form of teaching, such as a move to pupil-led discussion, does it?

> Perhaps not, but there are also other reasons to change our view of talk. Giving pupils greater ownership of their learning and creating a community of learners, for example. As it stands, teachers dominate classroom learning.

(Lefstein and Snell, 2011; Wells, 1999)

> That's as it should be. Teachers are the experts and it's their job to impart knowledge. Anyway, lessons these days are highly interactive, with plenty of questions put to pupils. They are far from passive.

> Certainly lessons may be superficially interactive, but the questioning and level of discussion often lack cognitive challenge. What's needed is a more dialogic classroom where pupils' collective reasoning is really allowed to come through.

(Alexander, 2017; Myhill, 2006)

> But isn't direct instruction, with fewer demands on working memory, a more effective way to teach? And anyway, sometimes a teacher simply needs to explain a new concept, surely?

That's a fair point. Sometimes a teacher does have to be more directive. So perhaps it's about knowing when to allow this freedom. It's less about strict adherence to a particular form of interaction and more about an overarching ethos.

(Alexander, 2017; Mortimer and Scott, 2003)

Even so, this seems like a challenging classroom environment to manage. For example, if we leave pupils to talk to their peers in groups, they'll quickly go off-task and either argue or just chat and they won't learn anything.

You're right that peer talk can easily be unproductive. The key is to teach pupils explicitly how to talk to one another and to set up tasks carefully that are conducive to this kind of learning. It isn't necessarily easy or an overnight transformation but it can be done.

(Mercer and Littleton, 2007; Mercer et al, 2017a)

But if pupils can learn to talk productively as peers in this way, where does that leave the teacher? Hasn't 'discovery' or minimally guided learning been called into question?

In some respects, yes. However, this does not imply a hands-off role for the teacher. Rather than merely facilitating learning from a distance, the teacher has a skilled and active role to play in modelling talk and providing structure for pupil dialogue.

(Gillies, 2016; Newman, 2017)

If I accept that this could be achieved, it still seems more efficient to have a largely teacher-led lesson. We can cover essential curriculum content much more quickly, for one thing.

> Maybe so, but the level of understanding might be more superficial. High quality talk has been shown to benefit not just reasoning but other outcomes. Anyway, isn't school about more than just academic attainment? There are multiple benefits for lifelong learning and well-being based on good spoken language and collaboration skills.

(Reznitskaya et al, 2009; Snowling et al, 2011)

> But is there actually good evidence that these benefits really transfer to other contexts beyond these talk-based lessons themselves? Improved reasoning is all very well, but teachers are judged on academic attainment.

> Good question. Until recently, a coherent evidence base has been somewhat lacking, but there is now a body of evidence showing transfer into other contexts and with impact on attainment in other subjects. More large-scale trials are now needed though.

(Alexander, 2018; Resnick and Schantz, 2015)

In this exchange, the three strands of argument from Section 1.2 are represented, but so too are very legitimate questions about issues such as principles of effective instruction, the demands placed on teachers and the impact on attainment. This provides a starting point for the consideration of the evidence in the rest of this book.

1.6 Organisation of the rest of the book

Chapter 2 provides the theoretical and empirical basis for an interest in class-room talk, exploring this from both cognitive and social perspectives. **Chapter 3** then considers what is known about patterns of whole-class interaction and how they can be developed further. Following this, **Chapter 4** seeks to develop your understanding of whole-class talk further by introducing the concept of dialogic teaching, a potentially powerful but challenging form of pedagogy. Shifting the focus from whole-class, teacher-initiated interaction to talk among pupils, the theme of **Chapter 5** is peer talk and collaboration, often in small groups. Having investigated the evidence for classroom talk in fairly generic terms, **Chapter 6** then focuses on how classroom talk relates to three aspects of learning for modern society: technology, metacognition and critical thinking. Finally, the complexity and diversity of educational environments mean that tailoring the principles from all of this evidence to specific settings is vital. With this in mind, **Chapter 7** is about implementing these ideas in practice through careful action planning.

Exploring further

This paper from Mercer and Dawes provides a useful summary of research in spoken language:

- Mercer, N and Dawes, L (2014) The Study of Talk between Teachers and Students from the 1970s until the 2010s. *Oxford Review of Education*, 40(4): 430–45.

The University of Cambridge has established the Hughes Hall Centre for Spoken Communication. Their website, including a video from Neil Mercer, provides an introduction to some of the arguments for spoken language in education:

- https://oracycambridge.org (accessed 17 May 2019).

Chapter 2
Learning as a social activity and the place of oracy

2.1 Chapter overview

This chapter will outline:

2.2 the ideas behind spoken language as a tool for learning;

2.3 why spoken language is so important in schools;

2.4 what is meant by the concept of oracy;

2.5 how oracy might be implemented across school.

2.2 What are the ideas behind spoken language as a tool for learning?

Theories of learning as a social activity

You will meet a number of key theorists in the chapters that follow, but the rationale for a classroom rich in talk is often traced back to two in particular: Jean Piaget and Lev Vygotsky. Better known for theories focused on individual development, rather than social aspects of learning, Piaget (1977) considers learning to arise from a constant need for cognitive equilibrium, or balance, in the face of new experiences. As part of this process, learning occurs through experiencing cognitive dissonance, or 'disturbance', leading to an imbalance and a shift in understanding. While often arising from independent engagement with the material world, this challenge to a child's thinking may also be induced by exposure to others' ideas, since contrasting views create a need to resolve the resulting imbalance (Piaget, 1950). The idea of 'socio-cognitive conflict' was developed further by Piaget's followers in a number of experiments (eg Mugny and Doise, 1978) and, as noted by Mercer (2000), spoken language can both create this conflict and be the means of resolving it. This productive consideration, through dialogue, of different perspectives is a key feature of Chapters 4 and 5. For Piaget, then, talk may be one of many routes to individual development.

For Vygotsky (1986), on the other hand, social interaction is at the very heart of learning. He suggests that speech has a communicative role in sharing knowledge, but also operates as an internal mode of thinking. In this sense, speech is functioning as both a cultural tool and a psychological tool respectively. As Higham et al (2014) explain: not only does dialogue underpin the process of learning to think, but meaning is co-constructed through this dialogue, rather than simply transmitted. Another of Vygotsky's important propositions is that adults might most productively focus not on what a child can already do independently, but on the potential that each child has when working with guidance. This fertile area of potential achievement, he terms the 'zone of proximal development' (ZPD). By interacting with a more capable partner, a learner develops new ways of thinking, for *what a child can do with assistance today she will be able to do by herself tomorrow* (Vygotsky, 1978, p 86). The implication, therefore, is that socially constructed learning, mediated largely through talk, is worthy of a good deal of teacher attention.

In seeking to integrate these two perspectives, Gillies (2016) distinguishes between personal and social constructivism. Both seek to explain how learners make sense of their experiences of the world, but Piaget's focus is on the *intra*personal, or individual development, while Vygotsky's is on the *inter*personal, or interaction between people. Rogoff (1990) similarly contrasts Piaget's interest in interaction as individuals sharing contrasting information, with Vygotsky's interest in interaction as a shared learning process in its own right. Edwards (2009) makes a further distinction between the social constructivism of Vygotsky, in which – for all the interest in interaction – a strong focus remains on outcomes for individuals, and a sociocultural interest in how learning and new understanding takes place *collaboratively*, at a group level. While social constructivism underpins much of this book, sociocultural theory is particularly relevant for Chapter 5 on peer talk. By way of drawing together these ideas, the twenty-first century has seen a surge of interest in educational implications of neuroscience. Goswami (2015) uses this evidence base to validate the key principles above, emphasising ideas such as: the socially mediated nature of children's learning, the crucial role of language in development and the need for dialogic as well as direct teaching. Talk-related implications for the classroom of these learning theories will already be apparent in, for example, the use of opportunities for speech to expose learners to contrasting ideas, the interest in structuring learners' next steps and the modelling of effective strategies just beyond a learner's reach. Nevertheless, it is important to remember that such connections are largely inferred, as the research of Piaget and Vygotsky was not carried out in classrooms. The next section considers the way these ideas have been extended into these settings by others, prefiguring many of the ideas to be encountered elsewhere in this book.

Educational application of the theory

Vygotsky's (1978) notion of the ZPD, under-developed at the time of his death, begs questions about precisely how pupils might be supported towards next steps in their learning and what form these interactions might take. These questions have often been taken up through the metaphor of scaffolding. Scaffolding is normally attributed to Wood et al (1976, p 90) who describe it as a process that:

Enables a child or novice to solve a problem, carry out a task or achieve a goal which would be beyond his unassisted efforts.

Bruner (1978), as part of this research team, further emphasises the central role in this process of verbal communication specifically in maintaining focus and progress. Through research on tutors supporting children 1–1 to complete a puzzle, Wood et al (1976, p 98) identify six forms of support that a more knowledgeable partner might give:

1. recruiting, or engaging the learner in the task;

2. reducing degrees of freedom by simplifying the task;

3. maintaining the learner's focus and direction;

4. marking critical features, through accentuating relevant aspects of a task;

5. controlling the learner's possible frustration;

6. demonstrating or modelling part of a task.

As can be seen, some of these forms involve minimal intervention, while others allow for more direction, as required. This is a reminder that the scaffolding metaphor is useful for its image of a temporary support but should not be seen to imply rigidity: scaffolding is about empowerment and a contingent, flexible response to a learner's progress. Wertsch (2008) has examined this as a transfer of responsibility. He shows how children move from 'other-regulation' by an adult to increased participation and 'self-regulation', culminating in moving beyond the ZPD altogether, as they take full ownership of a task through the internalisation of speech and thought. Wertsch suggests this progression ideally involves an adult skilfully tutoring a child in the problem-solving thought process itself through providing directions and modelling appropriate responses. The nature of scaffolding has also been examined by Van de Pol et al (2010) in a review of relevant literature. While many definitions exist, they identify three commonly accepted features, as shown below.

Table 2a Three features of scaffolding (adapted from Van de Pol et al, 2010)

Contingency	Responding and adapting to a pupil's changing needs, based on frequently determining a pupil's level of competence
Fading	Gradually withdrawing the scaffolding over time at an appropriate rate
Transfer of responsibility	Requiring the pupil to take increasing control of the activity, in both cognitive (task understanding) and metacognitive (process management) terms

Cazden (2001) points out that scaffolding does not only take place at an individual level. It can also be seen through skilled teacher involvement with groups – as will be seen at whole-class and small group levels in Chapters 4 and 5 – and through the structure and sequencing of curricular materials. While the literature therefore provides a measure of clarity over scaffolding and the potential role of talk, Howe and Abedin's (2013, p 342) systematic review of literature finds, from studies of teachers' actual practice: *'without exception, poor approximation to scaffolding is reported, together with considerable variation over what happens instead.'* It would seem, therefore, that effective scaffolding remains poorly implemented at classroom level and, according to Van de Pol et al (2010), under-researched in terms of its effectiveness.

Another way in which Vygotsky's ideas have been developed is to move beyond a view of socially mediated learning as a 1–1 interaction involving a more able party supporting a less able party. Mercer (2000) builds on the notion of the ZPD to introduce the concept of an 'intermental development zone' (IDZ). The IDZ explains how understanding is collaboratively constructed through joint activity and shared consciousness, allowing a focus on the variable contributions of all parties (Littleton and Mercer, 2013). As argued by Mercer and Littleton (2007), the IDZ also allows the idea of scaffolding and developing collective understanding to encompass potentially a small or even whole class group. In this sense, it links closely to the idea of the dialogic classroom which will be introduced in Chapter 4. Littleton and Mercer (2013) also use the term 'interthinking' to describe this application of talk, not merely to communicate but also as a tool for thinking collectively. Ways of promoting talk likely to lead to such interthinking are explored in Chapter 5.

A further elaboration on the learning from others in a ZPD comes from Rogoff (1990) who, like others cited in this section, views children as more active participants in learning than might have been implied in Vygotsky's (1978) work. Rogoff, however, also sees social interaction as a form of guided participation into society. The transfer of responsibility associated with scaffolding is conceived of as apprenticeship, going beyond the use of talk to include learning through tacit and non-verbal cues too. This apprenticeship involves: *'active learners in a community of people who support, challenge and guide novices as they increasingly participate in skilled, valued sociocultural activity'* (Rogoff, 1990, p 39). This perspective has much in common with others who have investigated learning as incremental participation in a community (eg Lave and Wenger, 1991). While Rogoff's research focuses much more on learning from parents or caregivers, as opposed to in-school settings, the idea of learning in a community is potentially powerful.

2.3 Why is spoken language so important in schools?

So far, the focus has been on the theoretical basis for talk chiefly as a tool, or medium, for learning. In addition to this, there is a line of argument for spoken language as an object of learning in its own right. Going back several decades, the influential Bullock report (Bullock, 1975), on behalf of the UK government, made clear – and still pertinent – recommendations for language assuming a high profile across the curriculum. Since then, however, spoken language has not always had a prominent position in curricula, despite initiatives such as the short-lived but influential National Oracy Project of 1987–1993 in the UK and international validation as one of the OECD's (2005) key competencies for success in modern society. Foremost among the current arguments for an emphasis on spoken language in classrooms is the link between speech and language proficiency and subsequent outcomes in education and beyond. This builds on a line of research from the 1970s onwards that, while valuing the richness of spoken language of children from low socio-economic groups, also highlights a potential mismatch with linguistic conventions within schools (Bernstein, 1971; Heath, 1983).

The 2008 Bercow Report for the UK government identifies communication as an essential, but neglected, life skill which provides the basis for social, emotional and educational development (Bercow, 2008). Drawing attention to communication as a basic *skill* in this way has led to the identification of striking deficiencies and inequalities. Speech, Language and Communications Needs (SLCN) can include: *'difficulties with fluency, forming sounds and words, formulating sentences, understanding what others say, and using language socially'* (Bercow, 2008, p 14). Research suggests up to 10 per cent of UK pupils may have SLCN (Centre for Social Justice, 2014) and clear predictive links have been made to later educational outcomes (Snowling et al, 2011). Beyond questions of academic attainment, SLCN are also seen as predictors of wider difficulties: research in the UK for the Early

Intervention Foundation charity (2017), for example, links SLCN to later mental health difficulties and involvement in the criminal justice system. SLCN are also over-represented in children from economically disadvantaged backgrounds, with a suggestion that the prevalence of SLCN within this group may be as high as 50 per cent (Centre for Social Justice, 2014). The Communication Trust, a UK coalition of organisations in this field, claims that while SLCN are on the rise, a large proportion of these needs remain unidentified (Communication Trust, 2013).

More generally, large gaps in children's vocabulary skills are seen between children from the richest and poorest families in the US as well as UK (Sutton Trust, 2012). Importantly, however, while teachers' perceptions of this 'word gap' are prominent in surveys (Oxford University Press, 2018), recent research adds another perspective. A US study by Gilkerson et al (2018) of the talk between parents and pre-school children suggests that adult–child *turn-taking* in talk is a stronger predictor of academic success years later than merely *exposure* to vocabulary. This provides another strong argument for teachers to focus on dialogue as a particular form of classroom talk. In all of these reports, it is important to note that it is not necessarily casual links that are claimed or established, but instead a strong correlation, within a complex social picture.

A further rationale for valuing talk as a form of language is provided by Carter (2003) and his extensive work on spoken grammar. Based on his study of a huge archive of spoken language recordings, Carter draws attention to the specific features and conventions of grammar in talk. While these are often distinct from written language, Carter places spoken and written grammar on the same continuum, particularly with the influence of modern technology and the hybrid genres of text messages and emails. Spoken language, therefore, is closely related to its written forms. Drawing on the same corpus of data, Carter (2004) also shows how talk can feature especially creative forms of language and thought. This serves not just a playful purpose, as heard in puns and figures of speech, but also a social and potentially critical one, as ideas are explored and there is a *'creative co-construction of relationships'* (Carter, 2004, p 188).

There are, therefore, compelling arguments for spoken communication being a fundamental skill needing to be taught explicitly. However, Cameron (2003) warns that a communication skills view of spoken language could result in a focus on a limited range of vocationally oriented tasks unlikely to generate either sophisticated speech or opportunities to learn through language. One concept that seeks to offer a more ambitious vision is that of oracy.

2.4 What is oracy?

Oracy is an idea attributed to Andrew Wilkinson (1965). He proposes the term as a description of ability in oral skills, including both speaking and listening, arguing for its teaching to be placed at the heart of schooling, alongside numeracy and literacy. The need for a specific term is justified in part by the power that words have to shape one's thinking (Wilkinson, 1970), implying that very naming of oracy might therefore raise awareness and confer status. More recently, Alexander (2012, p 10) defines oracy as:

> **What the school does to support the development of children's capacity to use speech to express their thoughts and communicate with others, in education and in life.**

Since the 1960s, other terms have been used in official documentation, including 'spoken language', 'oral language' and 'speaking and listening' (Millard and Menzies, 2016). Of these, 'speaking and listening' has been perhaps the most prevalent in the UK, but has been criticised for being conceptually weak and failing to address the complex relationship between the two components (Alexander, 2012). While Wilkinson's original conception of oracy suggests a focus on skills taught predominantly – though not exclusively – within the subject of English, others have developed the idea more broadly. The National Oracy Project sought to promote not only communication skills, but the use of speech and oral work as a means of learning (Norman, 1992), a view echoed in Edwards and Westgate's (1994, p 6) description of oracy as *'talking to learn'.*

Figure 2a Two aspects of oracy (Gaunt and Stott, 2019, p 9)

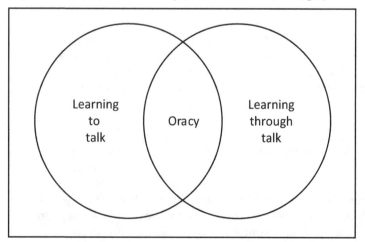

More recently, Voice 21, a UK group campaigning to raise the status of oracy in schools, has similarly proposed the model in Figure 2a.

While the interest in learning *through* talk, as well as *to* talk, is consistent with the focus of this book, oracy as a term is not always used in this way. Alexander (2012) makes a distinction between oracy, more narrowly, as the use of speech and what he calls 'oral pedagogy', as the use of talk as a medium for teaching and learning across the curriculum. Elsewhere, he draws on his international comparative studies to highlight also a similar polarisation in UK and US classrooms between social and cognitive functions of talk that is not found in some other countries (Alexander, 2003). While positive social attitudes to talk are a prerequisite for learning through talk, he identifies a need for an enhanced focus on the cognitive aspects, something that is taken up in Chapter 4's consideration of the dialogic classroom. Though Alexander (2012) argues that oracy and oral pedagogy are therefore intertwined and need to be considered together, Mercer (2018) advises caution. He suggests that the conflation of oracy education and what he calls dialogic teaching practices has led to a misconception among policy-makers that oracy is an optional pedagogical *strategy*, as opposed to essential curriculum *content*.

While 'oracy' as a specific term and unifying concept has been largely confined to the UK, the underlying ideas are evident – and sometimes more prominent – elsewhere in the world. This has been highlighted in Alexander's comparative work on primary schools, contrasting the UK with, for example, Russia (Alexander, 2000; 2003), and in many of the studies cited in the chapters to follow. Considering oracy directly, however, there are some signs of this term becoming used more widely. The English Speaking Union (2017), as strong advocates for this cause, report on an international meeting on 'oracy in global classrooms' attended by delegates from 22 countries, while the World Economic Forum's website also highlights oracy research, in a post making a case for its relevance internationally (McKenna, 2017).

2.5 How can oracy be implemented across a school?

While oracy is a powerful idea, its implementation varies considerably. Millard and Menzies (2016) carried out a survey on behalf of Voice 21 of over 900 teachers to find out about awareness of oracy, current practices and obstacles. Among their findings is that oracy is valued very highly, but that this is more pronounced among primary and early years teachers than those of older pupils. This links to Alexander's (2010) report of teachers' submissions to the Cambridge Primary Review calling for a greater prominence for oracy in the primary curriculum. Millard and Menzies' (2016) research also illustrates a number of challenges, however. Most staff members surveyed had not received recent training, teaching oracy explicitly across the curriculum remained inconsistent and a number of specific obstacles were identified. These included a lack of time due to curricular pressures, fears about pupils' behaviour or capabilities, teachers' own confidence levels and a perceived lack of support from school leaders. Similar challenges are raised by Coultas (2012), who notes dilemmas for teachers centred on practical issues around confidence and classroom management, but also judgments of peers and school leaders in a performative education environment.

All of this supports Mercer's (2015) argument that, if oracy is to attain a higher status in school, a degree of clarity is needed around the specific skills involved, including how they might be monitored or assessed. To this end, a University of Cambridge team has developed, through trials at a variety of schools with both primary and secondary pupils, a set of assessment tasks and an oracy skills framework providing relevant criteria (Mercer et al, 2017b). This is shown in Table 2b.

Table 2b Oracy skills framework (Mercer et al, 2017b, p 54)

Physical	Voice	• Fluency and pace of speech • Tonal variation • Clarity of pronunciation • Voice projection
	Body language	• Gesture and posture • Facial expression and eye contact
Linguistic	Vocabulary	• Appropriate vocabulary choice
	Language	• Register • Grammar
	Structure	• Structure and organisation of talk
	Rhetorical techniques	• Rhetorical techniques such as metaphor, humour, irony and mimicry
Cognitive	Content	• Choice of content to convey meaning and attention • Building on the views of others
	Clarifying and summarising	• Seeking information and clarification through questions • Summarising
	Self-regulation	• Maintaining focus on task • Time management
	Reasoning	• Giving reasons to support views • Critically examining ideas and views expressed
	Audience awareness	• Taking account of level of understanding of the audience
Social and emotional	Working with others	• Guiding or managing the interactions • Turn-taking
	Listening and responding	• Listening actively and responding appropriately
	Confidence in speaking	• Self-assurance • Liveliness and flair

A framework such as this, validated through research, provides a common language and understanding for schools promoting oracy. The broad, multi-dimensional model of oracy offers, particularly in its cognitive and social/emotional dimensions, a rich grounding for learning through talk across the curriculum. An important consideration, however, which might be associated with the linguistic dimension of a framework such as this, is the danger associated with over-emphasising a deficit view of spoken language. Coultas (2015), reviewing debates on spoken language in the UK, suggests that, alongside the development of talk as a 'democratic' form of pedagogy, there has also been a long-running strand of policy and practice seeking to *correct* language, based on notions of standard English. This relates to research from Fisher and Larkin (2008) who found negative judgments and low expectations about children's language to be prevalent among teachers. Fisher and Larkin's findings lead them to question the extent to which classroom talk is about conformity to a cultural norm, as opposed to a cognitive strategy, or whether *'disadvantage is less concerned with linguistic competence so much as linguistic difference'* (Fisher and Larkin, 2008 p 14). All of this points towards the balance required when implementing strategies to promote oracy, something which will be considered in the following case study.

Case study

Oracy at a whole-school level

Woodside Academy is an inner-city primary school. Rachel, the assistant head, heard about and joined a national training programme for oracy and began to work with her school team to embed these principles across the school. As well as the desire to improve the use of talk as a form of pedagogy, there was a strong commitment to raising aspirations and life opportunities for pupils through improving their confidence in communication.

For this to have serious impact, a shift of whole-school culture was needed and so the change had to be carefully implemented. It was important early on to build on relevant aspects of practice already in place, such as rehearsing writing through talk, and to focus on opportunities for relatively straightforward impact. An example of this was highlighting the immediate benefit for assessment for learning to be gained through allowing more time for pupils to share their thinking. New structures to support oracy objectives were introduced across the school: a four-part planning model helped teachers to consider the purpose for talk, its structure, the means of modelling and how it was to be reviewed.

While the substance of the taught curriculum was unchanged, it was important that oracy became an integral part of planning, so each year group had a specific oracy focus embedded into their termly topics. Year 2, for example, studied interviews and undertook a structured process of watching, deconstructing and planning for this form of talk, before finally being interviewed themselves. To avoid these developments being associated with just one school leader, a small number of teachers were initially invited to adopt and model these ideas in their classrooms. These teachers then allowed other colleagues to see techniques in practice, thereby acting as advocates and helping to build up staff confidence through their personal experiences and testimony. While a number of new strategies were introduced, based on ongoing training in this area, teacher judgment remained at the heart of pedagogical decisions, with an emphasis on talk strategies based on fulfilling a clear learning purpose.

A key part of this journey involved embedding oracy values in all that the school did. Each class negotiated a talk charter and reflected vocabulary for talk in its displays. At whole-school level, regular oracy assemblies were held, featuring pupil rather than teacher input. Using a four-part model based on the Cambridge framework in Table 2b, specific oracy assessment criteria for each year group were created, giving teachers a clear idea of relevant teaching points. The focus also extended to incorporating oracy targets into the annual performance management process, giving the initiative high status and emphasising strategic commitment from the top of the school. With oracy held as a core value, other new initiatives were evaluated with this in mind and implemented in line with these principles.

This case illustrates a number of important features, such as the need to provide clear structures and tools for teachers, focusing on gradual implementation. Above all, however, it shows the significance of embedding and explicitly valuing talk, not only across the curriculum, but in all aspects of school life and involving the entire teaching and leadership staff.

2.6 Summary

Talk in the classroom is underpinned by theories suggesting the value of exposure to diverse alternative perspectives and of talk as a tool for thinking and learning with others, but also for mediating one's own thought processes. Ideas such as scaffolding have sought to elaborate on these processes in an educational context, showing how this involves skilled and responsive interaction on the part of the teacher. As well as these arguments for socially mediated forms of learning, another justification for the prominence of classroom talk is the need to develop spoken language among pupils as the basis for successful outcomes in education and beyond. The concept of oracy draws attention to spoken communication as a key, but under-emphasised skill to be taught explicitly and this involves a number of dimensions, including the cognitive. While there are arguments for distinguishing between oracy and oral pedagogy, the two are intertwined and the former provides a strong grounding for the latter.

Questions for enquiry in your own school

- How is learning in your classroom scaffolded through opportunities for talk with either adults or peers?

- Based on a model such as the oracy skills framework, where in lessons might there be opportunities to develop the four strands?

- Which curriculum areas lend themselves well to particular aspects of oracy?

- How might your planning process or recording be amended to incorporate oracy?

Exploring further

The oracy skills framework and many examples for classroom implementation are outlined in this book:

- Gaunt, A and Stott, A (2019) *Transform Teaching and Learning Through Talk: The Oracy Imperative*. London: Rowman and Littlefield.

Voice 21's site includes resources, videos and other tools to help promote oracy in schools:

- www.voice21.org (accessed 17 May 2019).

Chapter 3
Whole-class interaction

3.1 Chapter overview

This chapter will outline:

3.2   an introduction to whole-class interaction;

3.3   what is meant by whole-class interaction;

3.4   the dominant whole-class pattern of talk;

3.5   how this typical pattern can be extended and enhanced;

3.6   how teachers can move beyond this pattern in whole-class interaction.

3.2 Introduction

Managing talk at a whole-class level is an everyday feature of any teacher's repertoire. The sheer complexity of simultaneous, multi-layered interactions, both verbal and non-verbal, can be challenging for even the most experienced practitioner. It is little wonder, then, that there is a widely noted tendency to keep things straightforward, predictable and controlled. This chapter explores the common features of whole-class talk and considers some of the typical and inherent constraints. Even standard, potentially restricted patterns of interaction, however, need not necessarily be cognitively limiting for the learner. There is scope to extend everyday practice in a variety of ways and a number of these adaptions are explored and evaluated.

3.3 What is meant by whole-class interaction?

Underlying the question of what is meant by interaction are others concerning who is doing the talking, when and why. Despite school rhetoric frequently implying that classroom interaction has a high status, it is very clear that particular forms of teacher-directed interaction prevail and that these have implications for the learning that takes place.

A long line of research, particularly from the 1960s onwards, has noted the 'asymmetry' of classroom interaction and particularly the way that talk is dominated by the teacher. Flanders' (1961) systematic observation examined patterns of teacher interaction in US classrooms over six years and famously derived from this the 'two-thirds rule': two-thirds of classroom time involves talk; two-thirds of that talk is teacher talk and two-thirds of teacher talk is a teacher explaining or directing. 'Superior' teachers were characterised by lower ratios of teacher talk and a greater focus on interacting with students' ideas. While Flanders' work is more than half a century old, these patterns have remained remarkably consistent over the years. Edwards and Furlong's (1978) seminal study of secondary school classrooms showed the way that talk patterns, often based on telling, reflected the teacher's authority. Galton et al (1980) gathered extensive primary classroom data in the UK over five years in the 1970s and noted interaction mainly at an individual level but with very little attention for each pupil. When they replicated their own work 20 years later, after the introduction of the national curriculum and its prescribed content, there was much more whole-class talk but in other respects little had changed in the intervening period: *'As was the case 20 years ago, teachers talk* at *rather than* with *children during class teaching'* (Galton et al, 1999, p 34).

Moving into the twenty-first century, researchers investigating the explicit emphasis on 'whole-class interactive teaching' in the National Literacy and Numeracy Strategies introduced to English primary schools, found that highly controlled, teacher-led talk continued to prevail (Burns and Myhill, 2004; Mroz et al, 2000). Indeed, computer-assisted analysis of video footage by Smith et al (2004) put the figure at 74 per cent teacher talk, suggesting that top-down initiatives like these strategies have little impact on underlying pedagogical habits. More recent studies with various ages of learner (Wangru, 2016; Vaish, 2008) paint a similar picture of teachers dominating classroom interaction, even when skilfully orchestrating classroom dialogue (eg Skidmore and Murakami, 2012).

This sort of asymmetry has important implications for learning. In such interactions, it may be the teachers and not the pupils who are doing most of the academic work, a marked contrast to the social constructivist ideas discussed in Chapter 2. As Hattie (2012) argues, teachers need to learn to listen much more, partly to allow pupils to deepen their thinking and partly to find out more about their pupils' understanding. His studies of effect sizes based on extensive meta-analysis show clear advantages for a high profile teacher role, but in the guise of an *activator*, guiding and involving pupils in their own learning. Related to this are questions of power, ownership of learning and communicative rights. Maybin (2006) describes the teacher's voice as an 'authoritative text' that frames social interaction in the classroom, suggesting that teacher-dominated talk serves to reinforce the hierarchy of the school.

As you can see, therefore, it is not interaction itself that is important, but its quality. Re-evaluating the word 'interactive' in the classroom context, Myhill (2006) makes a case for focusing on involvement and participation and

Alexander (2017) reminds us that it is not the organisational aspects of talk that matter, but rather the *discourse* and *values* associated with that talk. Alexander's research into types of teaching talk suggests a particular value for discussion and dialogue, but first the more commonly encountered forms and particularly what is often known as the recitation script must be examined

3.4 What is the dominant whole-class pattern of talk and why?

Extensive research worldwide has noted the near-ubiquity of what has been termed the Initiation, Response, Feedback (IRF) sequence. This can be a potentially limiting type of interaction, but one that can be enhanced in a number of ways.

The IRF pattern

The identification of IRF sequences is usually attributed to Sinclair and Coulthard (1975) who developed a framework for analysing classroom interaction in terms of three moves: an initiation by the teacher, a response from a pupil and feedback from the teacher. In its simplest form, IRF may be a very limited exchange indeed:

'What is the square root of 144?'

'12'

'Great, well done'.

This sort of interaction has also been characterised as triadic dialogue (Lemke, 1990) and as IRE (Initiation, Reply, Evaluation) by Mehan (1979). Mehan's emphasis here is that evaluation is the distinctive third move in *instructional* – as opposed to everyday – questioning. This basic pattern has been noted extensively in research across the world, as evidenced by Howe and Abedin's (2013) systematic review of 225 studies over four decades. Howe and Abedin point out that, despite some variation, this seems to cut across cultures, supporting Alexander's (2000) detailed observations of this phenomenon in five different countries and Hardman's (2008) reports on Nigerian and Kenyan classrooms. The persistence of IRF has been attributed by Mercer and Dawes (2008) partly to the implicit 'ground rules' that exist in classrooms, such as the teacher's exclusive right to evaluate pupil comments. Mercer and Dawes argue that ground rules are important but that new rules may be needed for different purposes. While Sinclair and Coulthard's original interest in IRF was purely as a linguistic exploration, the prevalence of this form of exchange raises a number of pedagogical questions for teachers. In examining three of these in particular, it is important to be mindful of Wells' (1999) point that an IRF structure is not inherently good or bad: rather, its value depends on the purposes it serves.

What are the issues for learning arising from the IRF pattern?

One frequent finding from research has been the association of IRF with a very limited repertoire of questioning. This is exemplified by a cluster of studies of primary classrooms in the UK in the wake of the literacy and numeracy strategies. Myhill (2006) report that over 60 per cent of questions were factual, rather than procedural, speculative or process-oriented and that children's own questions were seldom heard. Other researchers suggest that 70 per cent of children's responses were three words or fewer (Smith et al, 2004) or that, in many cases, a feedback move was missing altogether, resulting in a sequence of initiation-response-initiation-response, with teachers barely listening to children's answers (Burns and Myhill, 2004). However, in contrast, more recent research involving 28 English primary schools finds evidence of frequent use of 'productive' forms of dialogue, such as elaboration, reasoning and querying (Vrikki et al, 2019), so it is important to retain a sense of perspective about overly pessimistic portrayals. While much of this work has been at primary level, similar patterns of often limited interaction emerge from research with secondary pupils, for example in Switzerland and Germany (Pauli and Reusser, 2015) and Singapore (Vaish, 2008).

While these teacher-dominated exchanges undoubtedly have some value – indeed, Maybin (2006) uses analysis of such transcripts to show how repetition can lead to productive appropriation of ideas – they also point to another form of asymmetry within the classroom. What is clear from the frequent accounts of tightly controlled interaction is that the direction of thought is often dictated by the teacher with a tendency to seek convergence on a particular 'correct' response. The third move – feedback or evaluation from the teacher – is the key to controlling the flow of interaction (Mehan and Cazden, 2015). Mroz et al (2000, p 382) attribute this to: 'The teacher's claim to prior knowledge of the subject content and right to control the pacing and sequencing of its transmission'.

As Myhill and Warren (2005) point out, a focus on a pre-determined path through a lesson, usually in the name of meeting a set objective, serves teachers' purposes, rather than pupils' learning needs. Similarly, O'Connor et al (2017) point to the sheer complexity of balancing a range of requirements such as: clarity and coherence, adequate representation of content, time and equitable participation. This frequently leads to a trade-off of priorities that ultimately results in this same convergence effect.

Participation in talk is another issue. In their analysis of UK primary classrooms, Burns and Myhill (2004) found variations in participation according to gender and achievement level: there was much more positive participation in IRF exchanges by girls and high-achieving pupils. However, these findings take into account only observable acts of participation, such as putting a hand up to answer, whereas participation may be silent as well as vocal. A study of US Grade 4–7 pupils by O'Connor et al (2017) found no link between the amount of spoken contribution and an individual's performance on tests, though they attributed this partly to teachers developing a culture of pupils listening and orientating to a speaker. This echoes findings reported by Cazden (2001) showing pupils from a lower socio-economic group being much less willing to speak than their peers but nevertheless proving to have learned just as much.

3.5 How can the IRF pattern be extended and enhanced?

So far, this chapter has focused on some of the limitations inherent in IRF, but there has been a great deal of work on how even this simplest form of exchange might be made more productive.

For example, Mercer (2000) has identified five, near universal, conversational techniques observed in classrooms around the world which may be effective in linking new learning to pupils' prior experiences: one important purpose for whole-class discussion. These are listed in Table 3a.

Table 3a Building the future from the past (adapted from Mercer, 2000)

Recaps	Briefly reviewing prior learning for pupils
Elicitations	Questioning pupils to encourage recall of prior learning
Repetitions	Repeating a pupil's response in either an affirming or questioning tone
Reformulations	Paraphrasing a pupil's response in a clearer or more relevant form
Exhortations	Emphasising the value or relevance of past experiences for current activities

Apart from recaps perhaps, the other four techniques are entirely consistent with the teacher's initiation or feedback moves within an IRF sequence but serve a strategic purpose. This leads to a consideration of how to enhance each of the IRF phases.

Initiation: what sort of questions might be most productive?

Although questioning is a major topic in its own right, extending beyond
the scope of this book, it is clear that certain questioning strategies might
particularly promote high quality pupil responses. Hattie's current list of effect
sizes for classroom interventions rates questioning relatively highly, for its
impact on student achievement (Visible Learning Plus, 2018), but it is clear that
this potential depends greatly on the form that questioning takes. As already
noted, the vast majority of questions in whole-class exchanges are of the
closed, factual variety (Myhill, 2006); children are given limited time to respond
(Cazden, 2001) and these responses, unsurprisingly, are extremely brief (Smith
et al, 2004). In these critiques of the limitations of IRF, however, there is a danger
of overlooking the very important role played by even these apparently cursory
interactions. Indeed, questioning based on factual recall has an important place
in classrooms as an immediate diagnostic form of assessment. It can form
part of a highly contingent view of lesson planning in which: *the elicitation,
identification and interpretation of evidence is an indispensable component of
effective instruction*' (Black and Wiliam, 2018, p 11). As an example, Wiliam (2013)
refers to 'hinge points' in lessons. These are moments when teachers need to
take stock swiftly and efficiently of every pupil's understanding and respond
flexibly on the spot. Even brief, closed questioning, therefore, can be strategic
and full of impact on learning.

However, it is questioning to promote thinking and more extended responses
that is of particular interest here. To this end, Mercer and Littleton (2007)
report on studies from the UK and Mexico which explored the relationship
between teachers' use of questioning and their pupils' attainment in reading
comprehension and mathematics. Teachers whose pupils attained highly on
these tests had three questioning characteristics.

1. Questioning went beyond factual recall to encompass probing for
   understanding with a view to adjusting subsequent teaching.

2. Problem-solving strategies were modelled and children were encouraged
   to make their own thought processes explicit in their responses.

3. Questioning encouraged pupils to take a more active role in the
   classroom through articulating their reasoning, exchanging ideas and
   supporting peers.

Building on this last point, an extensive analysis of lessons in US classrooms
by Nystrand et al (2003) highlights the power of 'authentic' questions: those
without a pre-determined answer and offering a range of responses. In
short, questioning from this perspective is a scaffolded interchange, geared

towards guiding learning and developing pupils' metacognitive awareness of this process. Wertsch (1991) has seen similar examples as a negotiation of perspective, whereby the teacher reformulates pupil responses and shifts the responsibility for learning in their direction.

This use of questioning to guide enquiry has been investigated with Indian Grade 7 science pupils by Kawalkar and Vijapurkar (2013) and, from their observations, they derive five types of question which are likely to promote enquiry. These questions operate not discretely, but as a *progression* chronologically and in terms of cognitive demand (see Table 3b).

Table 3b Teachers' enquiry questions (adapted from Kawalkar and Vijapurkar, 2013)

Type of question and strategy	Examples
1. Exploring prerequisites/setting the stage eg factual recall and eliciting prior experiences	*'Where...?'* *'What...?'* *'Can you think of an example of...?'*
2. Generating ideas and explanations eg directing attention and asking for explanations	*'Did you see...?* *'How does...?'* *'Ask a question about...'*
3. Probing further eg asking for clarification, elaboration or justification	*'So, what would happen if ...?'* *'How do you know?'* *'How can that be?'*
4. Refining conceptions and explanations eg encouraging reasoning, making connections, pointing out flaws in arguments	*'How can we find out?'* *'So what was the difference between...?'* *'Why did we...?'*
5. Guiding the entire class towards scientific concepts eg encouraging wider responses, rephrasing, taking stock	*'Do you agree with...?'* *'How many of you...?'* *'X thinks...How do we know?'*

While this typology is a useful summary of questioning strategies designed to develop children's thinking, it is notable that this comes from lessons on science, a subject in which enquiry is an inherent feature. This sort of progressive questioning may be harder to implement elsewhere in the curriculum.

Response: how can you enable pupils to provide high quality answers?

Some researchers have focused on maximising the amount of participation by individual pupils through different response strategies, often aimed at challenging the convention of a small number of participants raising hands to speak. Wiliam (2006), for example, advocates a 'pedagogy of engagement', based on strategies requiring every pupil to participate, in order that their understanding be revealed and next steps considered. Our interest, however, is more on the *quality* of responses to teacher questions. One research focus has been the concept of 'wait time': the interval between the teacher asking a question and the pupil responding, or between an initial response and any follow-up. Some 40 years ago, Rowe's (1978) influential analysis of over 800 lessons showed a wide range of cognitive, social and affective improvements based on extending both forms of wait time to only around three seconds. Building on this, there is a now a strong consensus that such extension of these intervals can result in significant gains through encouraging wider participation and more sophisticated thought (Cazden, 2001; Loughran, 2010; Mercer and Dawes, 2008). However, Ingram and Elliott (2016), based on analysis of many classroom extracts, argue that teachers mechanistically increasing wait time may be counter-productive. They suggest that this perpetuates the artificial nature of teacher-dominated interaction and discourages the sort of natural, self-selecting participation more characteristic of everyday dialogue. Ingram and Elliott's view is that classrooms would be better served by teachers using their judgment flexibly and changing the norms and power imbalances within such exchanges. Similarly, Cazden (2001, p 82) has investigated ways of disrupting the teacher's *'role-given right to speak at any time and to any person',* providing examples of classrooms where pupils learn to manage their own turn-taking and teachers learn to listen more keenly.

In terms of who responds, Alexander's (2000; 2008) cross-cultural research calls into question the practice in places such as the UK and US of distributing brief questions to as many pupils as possible in the name of equity. He contrasts this with the very different patterns of participation found in Russian classrooms. Based partly on a more collective value system, fewer children participate in questioning, but they do so in a more sustained way, serving as representatives of the rest of the class and talking as much to their peers as the teacher. As well as enabling deeper forms of questioning, classroom talk again becomes as much about listening to others as competing to offer a brief 'correct' answer, an idea that accords with the point in 3.4 about the benefits of silent participation.

Feedback: how can the 'third move' be used for maximum benefit?

As you have seen, these exchanges have been represented as both IRF and IRE. Wells (1999) has argued that the third, follow-up, move is better thought of as *feedback* rather than evaluation, as this broader term offers greater scope for extending pupils' learning. In these triadic patterns, it is this feedback move that has the most influence on the quality of interaction (Wells and Arauz, 2006). This emphasis on rich feedback, rather than simply evaluation following a pupil's contribution, also relates to what is known more generally about feedback. Hattie's extensive meta-analysis has made clear the huge potential impact of feedback on attainment but also that this varies enormously, depending on how it is enacted. Effective feedback is focused on closing a gap towards a well-defined learning goal and should not be diluted with praise, or feedback at 'self' level (Hattie and Timperley, 2007; Hattie and Yates, 2014). Research on feedback in general is well summarised by Atherton (2018) in this series. More specifically and in view of current concerns about teacher workload, which centre partly on marking as written feedback (eg DfE, 2016; Elliott et al, 2016), there is an even more compelling case for high-quality, collective *verbal* feedback.

In line with this, a number of researchers have looked closely at teacher follow-up moves. Myhill and Warren's (2005) studies of 54 primary lesson episodes yielded three types of 'critical moment' as teacher moves shaped whole-class discussion:

1. moments of confusion caused by teacher misconceptions;

2. moments of careful steering of the class along a pre-determined path;

3. moments (more rarely) of flexible and responsive interaction, building on pupils' emerging learning.

This last category aligns with the productive discussions reported by Hardman (2008) in UK and African classrooms in which teachers created space for classroom discourse through strategies such as inviting pupils to comment on one another's ideas and asking for clarification, and thereby created a more symmetrical form of discourse. Greeno (2015) uses similar examples from US classroom transcripts to revisit the IRF abbreviation, noting variations like 'IRQA' to denote the follow-up questions and answers and 'IRRF' for a restating of the pupil response followed by a fellow pupil's feedback comment. Mehan and Cazden (2015, p 19) see these moves as a shift '*from recitation to reasoning*' and identify, from examples of science and mathematics lessons in the US, productive third move strategies such as:

- asking for clarification;

- expecting pupils to justify their reasoning;

- reformulating pupils' answers;

- seeking answers offering competing interpretations;

- allowing a number of responses before offering any evaluative comment.

The common factor here, then, is the extension of the third move. It is clear to see, therefore, that a narrow view of IRF as an isolated exchange between a teacher and one pupil may be unhelpful: one such exchange may well be part of a complex and potentially productive sequence of learning involving many moves and many pupils. Indeed, Molinari et al's (2013) analysis of Italian classrooms shows the prevalence of *chains* of IRF interactions, some of which go beyond a simple feedback on the appropriateness of the answer and instead offer opportunities for fruitful co-construction of understanding. Nevertheless, this move from convergence to divergence needs to be balanced against curriculum coverage and, as Skidmore and Murakami (2012) point out, orchestrating such discussions valuing contrasting viewpoints is a complex and dynamic balancing act for practitioners.

Case study

A teacher develops her questioning practice

Jane has a class of six and seven year-olds and is starting a unit of work on picture graphs in mathematics. Her usual practice when introducing a new topic is to do so with a mixture of teacher exposition – based on a structured sequence of slides – and questioning. Her colleagues have begun to film their own practice as a form of professional development and Jane has just done so for the first time. Although she has previously considered her whole-class episodes with pupils reasonably interactive and engaging, Jane is surprised to see that she has dominated the discussion and that her questioning has lacked purpose: on the one hand, the questions have lacked the precision and participation to be useful as assessments; on the other, they have failed to provoke deep thought. She resolves to use the next whole-class episode as an opportunity for deeper learning. The lesson begins in this way:

Table 3c Lesson and commentary

Interactions	Commentary and rationale
Jane shows the class a variety of objects seemingly from her desk drawer (pens, paperclips, pins etc) and asks, *'I need to sort out this mess. How can I quickly work out how many of each I have?'* She asks pupils to discuss this briefly with a partner.	Jane begins with an authentic, open question, allowing for a range of responses which help her to gauge starting points. By avoiding her usual hands-up mode of response, she has given each child a voice and audience and has effectively built in wait time before a public, formal response.
Jane then asks, *'What ideas did you and your partner have?'* Lots of hands are raised.	Jane phrases this question as an assumption that there will be ideas and offers children the safety-net of articulating their joint thinking, rather than just their own idea.
Raj is chosen and says, *'You could put them into different groups.'* Jane replies, *'Ah, I see. And why would you do that? Tell me more.'* Raj responds, *'So you can count them separately and see how many of each.'* Jane asks Raj to come and show her how he would begin to do this, scaffolding his explanation to the class as he does so.	Jane avoids a simple evaluation of Raj's answer and presses him in two ways to articulate his reasoning. She is conscious that Raj is having a turn while others are not, but decides a sustained response is worthwhile, so long as she and Raj are addressing the rest of the class with their comments.
When Raj has demonstrated counting and sorting into untidy piles, Jane asks, *'Can anyone build on what Raj just did for us, so that we can see more clearly how many there are?'* She pauses for a second or two before choosing Kelly to reply.	Jane consciously refrains from closing down the ideas with her views and offers another turn to the class. By using the words 'us' and 'build', she signals that this is both a collective and a cumulative effort.

(Continued overleaf)

Interactions	Commentary and rationale
Kelly suggests sorting the objects into orderly lines. Jane does so on her behalf, but not in size order, and adds, *'Like this? Is there anything else we can do?'* Alfie volunteers an idea: *'The objects could be lined up next to each other with the one with the most first and then the next biggest.'*	Jane has responded in a minimal way and deliberately left room for a further refinement of the children's thinking as part of the chain.
Jane follows this guidance and asks the whole class to count up the total in each line with her. She adds a sticker to record this number in each case. Together, Jane and the class have created a concrete version of a rudimentary picture graph. Jane then proceeds to link this to a visual representation of a similar problem...	The choral counting reinforces the collaborative reasoning and Jane acts as the conduit for the children's ideas. She has gradually refined their early explanations and guided them towards a more mathematical representation of the data.

What this example illustrates is a teacher stepping beyond a typical IRF exchange to develop a form of questioning that prompts children to think deeply but also collectively about an authentic question. Structure and purpose remain but feedback has become less evaluative and more empowering.

3.6 How can teachers move beyond IRF in whole-class interaction?

Other researchers have gone beyond an IRF-based analysis to consider patterns of productive whole-class talk more broadly. One of the most complete frameworks is the work of Michaels et al (2008) on what they have termed 'accountable talk', an analysis based on many years of research across a wide range of age groups. In this view, academically productive talk is characterised by three interrelated critical features, all of which must be present (see Table 3d).

Table 3d Accountable talk (adapted from Michaels et al, 2008)

Accountability to the learning community	Talk that takes into account and builds on others' contributions
Accountability to standards of reasoning	Talk that emphasises logical connections and reasonable conclusions
Accountability to knowledge	Talk that is based explicitly on facts and evidence

These principles have been exemplified for teachers through the development of a number of 'talk moves' (Michaels and O'Connor, 2015) in the form of prompts or other strategies, such as re-voicing, which is designed to model and nurture appropriate responses. An interesting aspect of this model is its emphasis on a firm knowledge base, at a time when there is widespread interest in knowledge-rich curricula (Young, 2013). Much of the other research examined, while not necessarily downplaying knowledge, has a greater focus on inquiry and thought processes, whereas this model is predicated on good reasoning underpinned by good knowledge.

Characterising talk moves is also a feature of the work of Tytler and Aranda (2015) who investigate the way that whole-class discussion is managed by primary teachers regarded as experts in Australia, Germany and Taiwan. Despite substantial differences in teaching approach, they identify a common 'discursive moves framework' of three productive moves:

- eliciting and acknowledging: canvassing new ideas;
- clarifying: sharpening ideas for greater precision;
- extending: seeking further justification and reasoning.

The fact that these categories are thought of as *moves,* rather than simply question types, hints at the complex and contingent interplay with learners. This work is of interest for its attempt to identify hallmarks of expert interaction that cut across cultures and pedagogical norms. The Taiwanese classroom, for example, had a far higher percentage of teacher talk and pupils were strongly led through a highly structured curriculum, but the same features were observable nonetheless.

While some studies measure success as quality of discussion, with an assumption, drawn from wider sociocultural theory, that this will lead to productive learning, there have been some attempts to link high quality whole-class discussion to pupil attainment more directly. A large scale study of US middle- and high-school pupils presented by Applebee et al (2003) reports a significant correlation between discussion-based teaching approaches and attainment on literacy tests. It is important to note that, while the benefits were seen for pupils of all attainment levels, those in the lowest tracks or streams were much less likely to encounter this form of pedagogy. All of this suggests the creation of a learning culture and norms of discussion that are much more collective and cumulative, pointing towards what has been termed 'dialogic' teaching and learning: the subject of the next chapter.

3.7 Summary

Whole-class interaction is often characterised by asymmetries of talk, with teachers dominating the exchanges. A long tradition of research across the world points to the resilience of the IRF pattern in a variety of forms. While often employed in a very limiting form, this need not be the case. There are examples of how teachers can make much better use of initiation and response practices to promote high level thought and participation. The third move, feedback, is particularly powerful if used to build on pupils' responses, rather than evaluating them in a closed manner. Some researchers have attempted to capture good practice in whole-class discussion in forms that go beyond a simple IRF analysis and these suggest a shift in classroom norms hinting at a more collective view of talk.

- Based on the critique of the term 'interaction' in this chapter, to what extent is your classroom truly interactive?

- How might your whole-class discussions move beyond always converging on a pre-determined outcome?

- What can you do to ensure that your follow-up to pupils' responses takes the form of productive feedback, rather than narrow evaluation?

- How do you seek to guide pupils' thinking through your discursive moves?

Exploring further

This paper sums up many of the issues surrounding whole-class interaction and its limitations:

- Myhill, D (2006) Talk, Talk, Talk: Teaching and Learning in Whole-Class Discourse. *Research Papers in Education*, 21(1): 19–41.

This chapter provides a useful overview of the research over the years on IRF and IRE patterns:

- Mehan, H and Cazden, C (2015) The Study of Classroom Discourse: Early History and Current Developments. In Resnick, L, Asterhan, C and Clarke, S (eds) *Socializing Intelligence Through Academic Talk and Dialogue*. Washington: AERA: 13–34.

This University of Cambridge site, focusing on active learning for all ages in mathematics and science, has classroom ideas and resources that may initiate productive whole-class interaction.

- https://inquiryproject.terc.edu/shared/pd/TalkScience_Primer.pdf (accessed 29 August 2019).

Chapter 4
The dialogic classroom

4.1 Chapter overview

This chapter will outline:

4.2 Introduction

In Chapter 3, patterns of talk were examined and some productive teacher 'moves' identified. There is a danger at this point, however, that the *function* of productive dialogue becomes exclusively associated with certain *forms* of talk. In this chapter, you will encounter the concept of a dialogic classroom framed as a broad set of values and practices, rather than a single, narrowly defined talk repertoire. A dialogic classroom is seen by some as an end in itself, based on the democratic value system it implies; for others, it is the means to greater reasoning and articulation of ideas; for others still, arguments can be made about the transferable learning and impact on subsequent attainment. This chapter critically explores the ideas and evidence behind all of these perspectives.

4.3 What is meant by 'dialogic'?

Dialogic teaching and learning is a broad heading which encompasses a range of similar approaches and practices. While chiefly associated in the UK with the work of Robin Alexander (2017), there are similarities with other bodies of research. From the UK, for example, there are overlaps with 'exploratory talk' (Mercer and Dawes, 2008) and from North America with 'collaborative reasoning' (Reznitskaya et al, 2009), 'dialogic inquiry' (Wells, 1999) and the notion of 'accountable talk' (Michaels et al, 2008) encountered in Chapter 3. What is common to all is that they articulate a classroom ethos that goes beyond talk itself to consider other classroom attributes (Calcagni and Lago, 2018). While dialogic practices are usually presented in contrast to the prevailing habits of interaction, it is important to note that some proponents argue that teacher-led forms of interaction retain an important role, since function, rather than form, is the defining characteristic of dialogic talk (Kim and Wilkinson, 2019). The focus, therefore, is more about the broadening of repertoires than about imposing a kind of orthodoxy.

As a way of starting to understand this concept, Maybin (2006) makes a helpful distinction between 'dialogue', as a word for conversation, and 'dialogic', which goes further to refer to the *'constant ongoing process of interactive and recursive meaning-making among children'* (p 24). Current understanding of dialogic processes is commonly associated with the influence of the Russian scholar Mikhail Bakhtin. Bakhtin's contribution includes his suggestion that any utterance is part of a chain of speech communication (Bakhtin, 1986), emphasising a connection not only with preceding utterances, but also with those to follow. This orientation to, and awareness of, an anticipated audience and response he characterises as 'addressivity' and all utterances, therefore, are seen as interlinked. Even when superficially monological, as when conveying an idea, they have the potential dialogically to create new meaning (Bakhtin, 1981, 1986). This meaning-making thrives in part on the existence of diverse perspectives and the tension between them, or 'dialogic gap' (Wegerif, 2011). Wertsch (1991, p 63), building on Bakhtin's ideas, points out that a fundamentally Bakhtinian question might therefore be: *'who is doing the talking?'* – the answer always being: *'at least two voices'*, since all speech has retrospective and prospective reference points to other voices. 'Dialogic' is a broad term, therefore, which is more about inter-connectedness and co-construction than just talk itself.

What may be clear from these points is that, as well as the arguments for academic and social benefit, explored later in this chapter, dialogic teaching implies a particular value system. One perspective on this might be the need to equip pupils for twenty-first century life in terms of citizenship and lifelong learning (Alexander, 2017), or a commitment to reasoned discourse (Reznitskaya et al, 2009). Another justification is provided by a desire to avoid a controlling, oppressive version of schooling characterised by Freire (1970) as 'banking education'. In contrast to this model of knowledge handed down to passive recipients, dialogic teaching is associated with pupil involvement in decisions and a more egalitarian environment. An important point in this respect, however, is made by Reznitskaya and Gregory (2013) who argue that this shared control need not diminish the teacher's authority as the more knowledgeable partner; in contrast it gives teachers the opportunity to demonstrate how their expertise may have arisen from their own participation in collective learning.

Dialogic teaching, therefore, needs to be understood holistically, as a habit of mind that goes beyond improved talk (Alexander, 2018). By way of summary, Lefstein and Snell (2011) suggest that a dialogic view of education offers a critique of traditional practice along five dimensions:

- structural: questions of whose voice dominates in classroom exchanges;

- epistemic: questions of knowledge as either accepted or contested;

- interpersonal: questions of individual versus collaborative approaches to learning;

- substantive: questions of the coherence and connectedness of what is learned;

- political: questions of power relations and authority in the classroom.

The next section explores what this shift in emphasis and these principles might mean at classroom level.

4.4 What are the hallmarks of the dialogic classroom?

Dialogic classroom features

Alexander (2017, p 23) stresses that specific forms of lesson or classroom organisation are much less important than *the quality, dynamics and content of talk* but it is clear that there are recognisable hallmarks of a dialogic classroom.

Originating in his large-scale comparative studies of pedagogy in classrooms in different countries (Alexander, 2000), Alexander (2017) offers perhaps the best-known list of dialogic teaching features, as seen in Table 4a.

Table 4a Features of dialogic teaching (adapted from Alexander, 2017)

Collective	Teacher and pupils addressing learning tasks together rather than in isolation
Reciprocal	Teachers and pupils listening, sharing ideas and considering multiple viewpoints
Supportive	Children sharing ideas without fear in a supportive environment geared towards helping with misunderstandings
Cumulative	Teacher and children build on one another's thinking and develop coherent chains of learning
Purposeful	Dialogic teaching is planned with particular educational goals in mind

Other definitions have added emphasis on implicit features of these classrooms, such as teachers and pupils addressing authentic, open problems (Snell and Lefstein, 2018) and the metacognitive aspects of learning (Reznitskaya and Gregory, 2013), through which pupils' awareness of these processes is explicitly developed.

It will be apparent that creating a dialogic environment is a complex undertaking. Alexander (2008) himself is clear that some of the observed international practices that inspired his vision of dialogic teaching are closely related to broader societal values, such as collectivism, which may be less common in countries like the UK and US. Creating the conditions for dialogic learning and teaching may involve a whole host of influences. The next sections explore two particularly important factors that help to distinguish further between dialogic teaching and interactive dialogue: communicative style and a sense of community.

Communicative style

It seems clear that a dialogic classroom must place special demands on a teacher's communicative style. An influential analytical tool has been developed by Mortimer and Scott through their study of talk in secondary science classrooms (Mortimer and Scott, 2003; Scott and Mortimer, 2006). Classroom interaction is examined along two dimensions (see Table 4b below). Using the first of them, dialogic discourse is contrasted with authoritative discourse, which allows for no deviation from the official, or 'textbook' content. Mortimer and Scott's insight is to use a second dimension – from interactive to non-interactive – to make a distinction between the degree of dialogic discourse and the degree of interaction. Teacher-dominated talk, therefore, may still have a dialogic quality, whereas a highly interactive exchange might remain entirely authoritative.

Table 4b Four classes of communicative approach (adapted from Mortimer and Scott, 2003)

	Interactive	Non-interactive
Dialogic	Interactive/Dialogic: *A range of diverse ideas is explored by teacher and pupils together*	Non-interactive/Dialogic: *The teacher summarises or explores different points of view without pupil input*
Authoritative	Interactive/Authoritative: *Pupils are highly involved through questioning but with a focus on one point of view*	Non-interactive/Authoritative: *The teacher presents a specific point of view without pupils' active participation*

The Interactive/Authoritative quadrant describes the more limited forms of IRF examined in Chapter 3 but perhaps most interesting is the Non-interactive/ Dialogic quadrant, allowing, for example, for teacher-led modelling of dialogic thought processes. Using analysis of science classroom transcripts, Scott and Mortimer (2006) show how teaching might be characterised by a series of skilful and productive *shifts* between dialogic and authoritative discourse. These shifts are not dictated solely by the teacher. In a dialogic classroom, pupils may pose high-level 'wonderment' questions, which sometimes act to shift the focus independently of the teacher (Aguiar et al, 2010). This interplay places great demands on a teacher's subject knowledge (Scott, 2008) and will vary depending on the discipline in question. As these researchers point out, dialogic discourse is valuable in terms of motivation and making connections but science, in particular, also depends to a certain extent on guidance towards authoritative forms of established scientific understanding, as illustrated in this chapter's case study.

A sense of community

If Mortimer and Scott's (2003) framework helps teachers to plan for *cumulative* and *purposeful* dialogic classrooms, another of Alexander's (2017) criteria – *collective* learning – has also been the subject of much research. While some have analysed learning in everyday settings through the lens of participation and apprenticeship (Lave and Wenger, 1991; Rogoff, 1990), this has often focused on the idea of a 'community of practice'. Subsequent researchers have often pointed out the limited transferability of this model to the school setting, with its often isolated and fluid working practices (Chambers and Armour, 2011; Wubbels, 2007).

In a review of research on classroom communities with learning, rather than practice, as their object, Watkins (2005) suggests that they result in: disciplined discourse, shared knowledge, co-constructed learning and shared metacognition. Yet another vision of community, which aligns even more clearly with dialogic teaching, has been proposed by Wells (1999) and his work on communities of *enquiry* in science classrooms, in which the main object of collaboration is not induction into practice or learning for its own sake. Instead, the object is the joint solving of a problem and the development of a metacognitive awareness of this process in *'a classroom community which shares a commitment to caring, collaboration and a dialogic mode of making meaning'* (Wells, 1999, p 334). Based on this model, Wells and Arauz (2006) report on research with Canadian teachers over a six year project aimed at creating such communities. They found that adopting a communal enquiry orientation in this way did result in a far more dialogic style of interaction, though this was often still within the triadic IRF pattern discussed in Chapter 3. This is attributed in part to the teacher's responsibility for guiding pupil engagement with a prescribed curriculum and still permits authentically dialogic teaching to occur. As well as the teacher's instructional role, Skidmore (2006) points towards the teacher's role in the *affective* aspects of a community, as a 'concerned other', guiding, coaching and sharing in the ups and downs of the discovery process.

A dialogic stance

What both of these bodies of research point towards, therefore, is a way of resolving the abiding tension between the need to ensure curriculum coverage and purposeful learning on the one hand with a commitment to a genuine co-construction of meaning on the other. As Mercer and Littleton (2007) point out, from their research in primary science lessons, it is the quality of the collective thinking *as a whole* that is important. Seen this way, the teacher judgment and shifts between dialogic and authoritative discourse, or the monologic episodes within a broader dialogic community noted above, are entirely compatible with a dialogic classroom. What this strongly suggests is that individual episodes of talk are less indicative of classroom culture than what Wells and Arauz (2006, p 418) call a *'dialogic stance'*.

The idea of a dialogic stance is taken up by Boyd and Markarian (2011) who use a close analysis of classroom talk to show how features such as didactic teacher comments or closed questions may still allow for a discourse space allowing pupils to have a genuine voice. Much of this depends on the readiness of the teacher to listen more attentively: when considering talk, *'it is not just how we say it, but how we are predisposed to receive it'* (Boyd and Markarian, 2011, p 516). A dialogic stance, then, has much in common with the creation of an 'intermental development zone' (IDZ) (Mercer, 2000), as introduced in Chapter 2: a shared space for truly collective thinking between teacher and pupils. The argument for dialogic teaching going beyond specific talk forms is also reinforced by Alexander (2017). His highly detailed list of indicators of dialogic teaching covers not only hallmarks of the talk itself, but many aspects of the wider context, including matters of organisation, pace, lesson structure and an awareness of the impact of teachers' dispositions and interventions. While it will be clear already that dialogic teaching may encompass all forms of classroom interaction, the focus of the rest of this chapter is primarily on specific practices for whole-class talk. Small group, peer interaction will be considered more specifically in Chapter 5.

4.5 What are the practices associated with dialogic teaching?

Based initially on his comparative studies of classrooms internationally and then refined through subsequent studies, Alexander (2017) identifies a series of repertoires that teachers need to use. These include organisational structures and opportunities for developing pupil talk for both everyday life and learning (eg narrating, explaining and negotiating). His other repertoire concerns teaching talk:

- rote: drilling of facts through repetition;

- recitation: questioning designed to stimulate recall of previous learning;

- exposition: imparting information;

- discussion: exchanging ideas;

- dialogue: achieving common understanding through cumulative questioning and discussion.

While Alexander is clear that all of these forms have their place, the first three often account for the bulk of classroom talk. The less frequently used last two – particularly dialogue – have the greatest cognitive potential and are the basis of enacting the dialogic principles set out in Section 4.4.

Related to this, Nystrand et al (2003, p 178) make a distinction between discussion as *open-ended conversational exchange of ideas largely absent of questions* and dialogue as *engaged student questions and an absence of teacher test questions*, noting that the two often overlap. However, in their analysis of extensive data gathered from over 200 US middle and high school classrooms, 79 per cent of observed episodes had neither discussion nor dialogue and only 2 per cent had both. These rare 'dialogic spells' were characterised by:

- increased interest and enthusiasm of pupils;

- discourse building on past contributions;

- pupils asking questions;

- teachers refraining from asking questions testing recall;
- pupils answering questions with little prompting or without being individually chosen.

A very different, but complementary, perspective to this large-scale quantitative analysis is provided by researchers such as Skidmore and Murakami (2012) who closely examine transcripts of dialogue to note the teacher's complex balancing act. This often involves initiation through a question or problem involving many possible viewpoints, the accommodation of pupils' diverse ideas and the maintenance of engagement in a collective exploration. Drawing on a wide range of qualitative studies, Reznitskaya and Gregory (2013) summarise characteristics of the talk within dialogic classrooms. They suggest that cognitive and linguistic tools for effective engagement in reasoned argumentation are developed through:

- teachers asking open-ended questions geared towards enquiry;
- pupils articulating a position on an issue and backing this up with reasoning;
- pupils making lengthy contributions, explaining their thinking;
- teachers and pupils engaging in meta-level talk, with reflection on dialogue itself;
- teachers providing meaningful feedback to prompt further enquiry;
- teachers building on pupils' answers and seeking elaboration;
- pupils building on their peers' contributions in coherent lines of inquiry, listening to one another and responding accordingly.

As you will see, there is a degree of consensus over these characteristics but they ask a great deal of the teacher's expertise. The next section explores what is known about achieving this goal.

4.6   What does research suggest about the impact of dialogic practices?

Practices found to promote dialogic talk

One way to consider and evaluate dialogic teaching is to accept the case made in Chapter 2 about the importance of talk in children's learning, as well as the value-based arguments introduced in this chapter, and to focus simply on evidence on promoting dialogic talk, presuming this to be a desirable outcome in its own right.

Some studies have focused on establishing dialogic practices in the classroom through structured programmes of intervention. For example, Alexander (2008) summarises findings from two research projects in London and Yorkshire with primary and lower secondary pupils. These projects (eg Alexander, 2004) used a combination of training, advisory work, documentation and video analysis in an attempt to embed dialogic talk across schools. While outcomes were somewhat mixed, often relating to fidelity to the programme, there were broadly positive developments in the quality of talk, such as extended contributions from pupils, less teacher direction and longer chains of interaction. As an example of a similar outcome, improvements in communicative competence among early years pupils were found in an experimental study involving a six week intervention in the Netherlands (Van der Veen et al, 2017). Notwithstanding the challenges also identified, these studies suggest that significant improvements in talking practice are achievable through a structured intervention project.

In contrast, Mercer et al (2009) conducted a study that raised participants' awareness of whole-class dialogic practices, but refrained from a formal programme of intervention. This yielded talk that was plentiful and often productive, but rarely met the criteria for dialogic interaction. Mercer et al (2009) contrast this more general talk with evidence of dialogic talk stimulated by what they call 'talking points', or provocative statements to debate (eg *The moon changes shape because it is in the shadow of the earth*'). This device has much in common with the 'concept cartoons' developed by Naylor and Keogh (2013) some 20 years ago, in which high quality dialogue is developed through presenting alternative viewpoints – including erroneous ones – on everyday situations related to scientific concepts. The implication is that a talk stimulus reflecting differing viewpoints may be particularly powerful.

Khong et al (2017), in a review of research on classroom talk, identify the creation of a culture of enquiry as one of three approaches taken to developing dialogic talk (the others being the training of teachers, as seen in this section, and the training of pupils, which will feature in Chapter 5). In an enquiry-based classroom, dialogic talk becomes a logical by-product of the curriculum itself. This model of learning through enquiry is often associated with Wells (1999) who proposed learning through a five-step process of:

1. responding to a launch (stimulus and elicitation of questions);

2. researching;

3. interpreting evidence;

4. presenting findings;

5. reflecting on the process.

As previously cited in 4.4, the data from extensive enquiry-oriented projects reported by Wells and Arauz (2006) suggests real benefits for dialogic talk. It is notable that Wells' data, like many other studies cited, comes from the science classroom. While his vision is a broader one, based on *'discipline-based forms of inquiry...in all areas of human activity'* (Wells, 1999, p 163), not all subjects are as inherently associated with enquiry. While there are examples of curricula beyond science which are organised around enquiry, such as the International Baccalaureate Organization's programmes (IBO, 2013), this remains relatively unusual.

Other researchers have focused on a close analysis of whole-class interaction to identify particular triggers for dialogic talk. Returning to the extensive quantitative analysis of English and social studies classrooms in the US by Nystrand et al (2003), certain teacher and pupil moves are found to be associated with creating the conditions for dialogic spells. These are outlined in Table 4c, using the analogy of building a fire.

Table 4c Three factors in dialogic discourse (adapted from Nystrand et al, 2003)

Teacher primes the class for dialogic discourse: the 'kindling'	Creating the conditions, for example by: • posing a provocative question; • soliciting ideas and opening up the floor; • withholding evaluation of ideas; • encouraging pupils to respond to one another.
Pupil respond in an engaged way: the 'spark'	Taking up the teacher's bid, for example by: • freely voicing their ideas; • asking their own questions; • building on others' questions to form clusters of pupil questions.
Open discussion breaks out: the 'ignition'	Critical discourse begins, for example featuring: • teacher and pupils co-constructing their understanding; • teacher stepping back and just keeping the discussion flowing; • questioning and transmitting information giving way to working out ideas jointly.

What this analogy highlights once again is the importance of creating a dialogic culture, rather than simply focusing on talk itself.

Dialogic talk and impact on attainment

It seems clear, then, that there is evidence for specific practices which promote dialogic forms of talk. However, a pertinent question, particularly in an international climate of competition, standardisation and accountability (Sahlberg, 2016), is whether there is firm evidence for the impact of dialogic teaching on *attainment* more directly. In the Van der Veen et al (2017) study mentioned in Section 4.6, for example, the improvements in communication were not accompanied by greater improvements in subject-matter knowledge in post-intervention tests. As Reznitskaya et al (2009) argue, large-scale, empirical evidence for the impact of dialogic approaches on educational outcomes beyond the quality of talk itself has been relatively scarce.

Some evidence for impact of dialogic approaches on attainment has been found in US classrooms. Applebee et al (2003) examined lesson footage of 974 pupils in Grades 7–11 across 19 schools, looking for any correlation between features of dialogic instruction and raised literacy attainment. Dialogic episodes were evidenced by:

- open discussion between at least three participants;
- authentic teacher questions without a pre-specified answer;
- uptake of a previous speaker's ideas.

These researchers found very consistent results (Applebee et al, 2003) relating high academic demand and discussion-based approaches to performance in literacy tests across a range of ages, pupil backgrounds and school types. Notable in both these examples is an emphasis not on the amount of talk, but on the quality of collective co-construction of meaning. More recently, O'Connor et al (2015) report on the findings of interventions in Grades 4–7 mathematics lessons. An initial large-scale, talk-rich intervention with some 500 pupils over four years led to significant improvements on subsequent tests. This was then probed further in a small-scale controlled study based on the sorts of 'talk moves' (Michaels and O'Connor, 2015) discussed in Chapter 3. Even when taught by the same teacher, pupils' attainment, when compared with traditional direct instruction, was significantly higher in the groups taught.

In the UK, Howe et al (2019) undertook a large study capturing naturally occurring talk in 72 primary classes and found two forms of teacher–pupil dialogue to be positively associated with performance on mathematics and English tests (though not on tests of science and reasoning), so long as pupil participation was also high. These two powerful forms of dialogue, seen by the authors as relatively straightforward and manageable for teachers to promote, were:

- elaboration: building on, elaborating, evaluating or clarifying a contribution;
- querying: doubting, disagreeing with, challenging or rejecting a statement.

It is notable that these forms have much in common with the categories of uptake and authentic questioning found by Applebee et al (2003), mentioned above.

Dialogic teaching has also been evaluated for its impact on attainment through a randomised control trial (RCT) in 38 UK schools as part of a wider evaluation project (EEF, 2017). The intervention, devised by Robin Alexander and based on his model of dialogic teaching (Alexander, 2017), featured a training programme and then a two term implementation in Year 5 classrooms. In subsequent tests, pupils in the intervention group made additional progress of two months in English and science and one month in mathematics. While Alexander's (2018) own reflections on the RCT highlight a number of methodological limitations, the results, achieved at relatively low cost, are encouraging nonetheless. Alongside these outcomes, however, comes recognition again that fully embedding dialogic teaching approaches requires longer-term engagement (EEF, 2017), a finding in line with previous arguments for an embedded dialogic classroom culture. While Alexander acknowledges that isolated elements of dialogic practice, or fairly brief interventions such as this, can have positive effects, he strongly asserts that dialogic teaching, in his conception, is a *'total pedagogy'* (Alexander, 2018, p 31) involving a more fundamental shift of values and practices.

There are also examples of pedagogical practices which, while not explicitly positioned as dialogic, nevertheless fulfil many of the same criteria. One such initiative is a series of research-based resources from King's College, London, aimed at 'cognitive acceleration' of pupils in mathematics and science. These programmes, such as Cognitive Acceleration through Science Education (CASE), are based on three principles: the Piagetian idea of cognitive conflict, Vygotskian social interaction and metacognitive reflection. Lessons feature subtly guided activities, beginning with concrete preparation and centred on conflict resolution through collaboration and dialogue, which are then linked, or 'bridged' into the broader science curriculum (Adey and Shayer, 2015). In terms of the commitment to enquiry, reasoning and co-construction of meaning through talk, CASE and its related programmes bear the hallmarks of dialogic teaching.

The effect on attainment of the resulting materials, published as *Thinking Science* (Adey et al, 2003) has been impressive. For example, Shayer (1999) reports on cohorts of pupils followed over several years who showed improvements in attainment that were sustained not only immediately after the CASE lessons, but in national tests two years after the intervention and which were evident in English and mathematics as well as science itself. Similar long-term and transferable impacts on attainment are reported from the subsequent Cognitive Acceleration in Mathematics Education (CAME) projects with both primary and secondary age groups (Adey and Shayer, 2015). Nevertheless, it is notable that, amidst their reports of success, it is clear that this is a substantial commitment: sustained use – the programmes are designed as two year interventions – and teacher professional development are essential to their success. Furthermore, challenges for teachers, as they probe for reasoning and steer discussions contingently may be considerable (Oliver and Venville, 2015). In the following case study, a teacher grapples with some of the challenges of implementing these cognitive acceleration principles within his lessons.

Case study

A science teacher begins to implement *Thinking Science*

Mark was a secondary-school science teacher. A few years into his career, he found himself becoming dissatisfied with his pupils' somewhat superficial approach to learning – often strategically focused on test performance – and was looking for ways to promote deeper thinking within his lessons. He heard from a local university about CASE and the *Thinking Science* materials, attended some training and decided to try this out in his Years 7, 8 and 9 biology classes. Mark proceeded cautiously at first, retaining much of his usual practice, but planning a few of his lessons each week based on the CASE principles (the intervention involved 30 lessons over two years).

Each lesson began with a challenging problem to consider, centring on a practical or concrete experience designed to induce a degree of cognitive conflict. CASE emphasises social construction of understanding, so Mark needed to plan for opportunities for talk and the sharing of pupils' ideas. He understood that he needed to allow pupils to direct their own enquiry through this discussion as they worked on the problems, but he initially found it difficult to refrain from offering answers and closing down the dialogue. At times, the awkward pauses, as he stopped himself from giving immediate feedback, were uncomfortable for teacher and pupils alike and it became clear that this sort of lesson would involve a shift in classroom culture that would take time.

Gradually, pupils became more accustomed to this form of interaction and their reasoning and awareness of the learning process were much more evident, but this presented a new challenge. Mark found that he was often having to improvise his responses and interventions rapidly, placing great demands on his subject knowledge, as lessons proceeded in unexpected directions. A further issue Mark encountered was that the freedom to work collaboratively and largely independently of the teacher gave potential for misconceptions to arise. As a result, Mark planned lessons around a series of shorter episodes, allowing authentic discussion but building in frequent plenary moments. These allowed him to draw together progress and help the class to reach a consensus reflecting correct scientific understanding, before moving onto a new phase of discussion. Towards the end of the first year, changes were already becoming evident. Mark had begun to incorporate some new habits into his 'traditional' lessons, allowing pupils more opportunity to struggle with their own explanations and discuss answers with peers. Pupils themselves saw value, not only in the *Thinking Science* lessons, but in their work across the curriculum.

Commentary

Mark's shifts of practice in this example have much in common with Alexander's (2017) vision of a dialogic classroom. A far more collective, reciprocal and supportive lesson format emerged, as pupils and teacher jointly considered these problems and more space was allowed for pupils' voices. The tensions Mark encountered relating to pupil misconceptions and his own subject knowledge relate in particular to Alexander's 'cumulative' and 'purposeful' criteria. What seems clear is that dialogic teaching requires fidelity to a programme and that long-term impact most likely involves a change of culture. This may be difficult to enact in the short-term or in isolation but, even in a diluted form, dialogic practices may seep quickly into other learning for both teachers and pupils. In the next section research on some of these issues is considered in more depth.

4.7 What are the challenges of dialogic teaching?

Despite the evidence for the benefits of dialogic teaching, it is also clear that this is far from straightforward to enact. Snell and Lefstein (2018) identify five key issues in their review of the research literature:

1. the lack of time in a crowded curriculum geared towards high-stakes tests;

2. the necessary culture shift in terms of views on knowledge, authority and learning;

3. the durability of existing practices;

4. the demands placed on teacher knowledge and flexibility;

5. the clash with embedded pupil identities, particularly around ability.

Challenges for the learner

Snell and Lefstein argue that there is a tension between the inclusive ideals of dialogic pedagogies and the tendency to label some pupils as low ability and incapable of rising to the cognitive challenges of the dialogic classroom. This is reinforced by Sedova et al (2014) whose research found only the most motivated and gifted pupils participating in this sort of talk. While Sedova et al suggest either withdrawing 'low-track' students or lowering the challenge level for all, this is called into question by the large-scale study by Applebee et al (2003) who found benefits of dialogic teaching for *all* levels of attainment. The key problem, they suggest is instead one of expectations and a lack of opportunity, as discussion-based approaches have not been widely tried for what they term 'lower track' pupils.

A further issue pertaining to all learners emerges from insights from cognitive science into the process of learning. Kirschner et al (2006), in a summary of research into instruction involving 'minimal guidance', claim that all forms of enquiry-based learning make heavy demands on working memory and that such approaches are largely ineffective for pupils learning new concepts. Novel information, they argue, needs to be taught explicitly through processes such as worked examples. One perspective on these ideas about memory is that of cognitive load theory. This implies that teachers need to minimise unnecessary, or 'extraneous', cognitive load in the form of, for example, redundant information or the need to attend to multiple sources of information (Sweller, 2016). It is immediately clear that this raises questions about the cultivation in a dialogic classroom of a community of enquiry with its potential for divergent collective thinking. However, it is all too easy for such debates to become polarised. The principles of introducing novel information through teacher-led instruction and grounding higher-level debate and thought in prerequisite prior knowledge are not incompatible with a broader dialogic approach. Indeed, they align with the shifts between authoritative and dialogic approaches discussed in Section 4.4 (Scott and Mortimer, 2006) and an assumption that effective enquiry is based on extensive teacher scaffolding (Hmelo-Silver et al, 2007). The main implication of these ideas, therefore, may be more about the choice of a communicative style fitting for a given stage in a learning sequence, rather than a binary choice between ideological positions.

Challenges for the teacher

As shown in Chapter 3, IRF is highly resilient. Reznitskaya and Gregory (2013) argue that, due to the patchiness of the research, teachers commonly under-estimate the challenges involved and so it is important to acknowledge these obstacles openly. With this awareness, Alexander (2017) proposes a constructive way forward. Rather than discussing deficits, Alexander re-frames them as *dilemmas*, often centred on striking a balance between approaches like questioning and telling, or open discussion and teacher-led discussion. Alexander argues that such matters of judgment concerning the form of talk have been shown through research to be amenable to change. He therefore divides his five fundamental principles into two groups. Three of the principles relate to this *form and culture* of talk: building collective, reciprocal and supportive classrooms; the other two – cumulative and purposeful – concern the *content* of talk. Achieving cumulative, and thereby purposeful, talk is, he suggests, often under-emphasised in research and is where the greatest challenges lie. Alexander therefore proposes a phased approach, as shown in Table 4d.

Table 4d A two phase process (adapted from Alexander, 2017)

Phase 1	Talk that is: • collective; • reciprocal; • supportive.	Establishing the conditions, by creating the appropriate ethos and dynamics
Phase 2	Talk that is: • cumulative; • purposeful.	Structuring and sequencing content to meaningful ends, through teachers' skilled and flexible responses and interventions

4.8 Summary

Dialogic teaching, for many, goes beyond talk to reflect a wider educational value-system centred on an egalitarian and participatory view of learning. It involves creating a classroom ethos based on dialogue, collective problem-solving and a co-construction of understanding. While classroom talk may at times need to be teacher-led and authoritative, a dialogic stance can nevertheless be maintained, based on a commitment to communal inquiry.

Dialogic talk can be developed effectively in schools through structured intervention programmes and can be initiated in classrooms through particular forms of stimulus. Dialogic teaching has been shown to have benefits, not just for the quality of talk itself, but for attainment in various subjects and pupils' metacognitive capacities. Nevertheless, it remains a challenging form of pedagogy to enact well.

Questions for enquiry in your own school

- What might you change in your school or classroom culture that would help to develop a 'dialogic stance' in the approach to the ownership of learning?

- Which aspects of the *forms* of dialogic talk covered in this chapter (collective, reciprocal and supportive) are already in evidence in your setting?

- Do pupils of all attainment levels have the same access to learning through high-quality discussion?

Exploring further

This paper by Robin Alexander offers a useful summary of his model of dialogic teaching, as well as the recent evaluation discussed in this chapter:

- Alexander, R (2018) Developing Dialogic Teaching: Genesis, Process, Trial. *Research Papers in Education*, 33(5): 561–98.

Robin Alexander's site has a multitude of links related to dialogic teaching:

- www.robinalexander.org.uk (accessed 17 May 2019).

The Let's Think website provides resources associated with cognitive acceleration, as discussed in the case study:

- www.letsthink.org.uk (accessed 17 May 2019).

Chapter 5
Promoting productive peer talk and collaboration

5.1 Chapter overview

This chapter will outline:

5.2   the different contexts for peer dialogue;

5.3   the different kinds of peer talk;

5.4   how pupils make sense together through peer talk;

5.5   the evidence for the benefits of peer talk;

5.6   how productive peer talk can be promoted;

5.7   the challenges associated with peer talk.

5.2 What are the different contexts for peer dialogue?

In Chapters 3 and 4, the focus has been mainly on whole-class interaction, but this represents only one of a number of modes of classroom talk. To go alongside the various forms of teaching talk introduced in the previous chapter, Alexander (2017) also offers, in his list of teachers' repertoires, a variety of organisational contexts for talk. As well as teacher–class and teacher–pupil interaction, he draws attention to:

- collective group work (teacher-led);
- collaborative group work (pupil-led);
- one-to-one (pupil pairs).

This chapter focuses on the interaction between pupils, which may be prompted to some extent by teachers, but is largely between peers, either in pairs or small groups. To return to the ideas introduced in Chapter 2, a distinction is made between a social constructivist interest in collaboration as the means to *individual* development and a sociocultural interest in collaboration in terms of *learning as a group* (Edwards, 2009). In the focus here on the latter, it is important to acknowledge that not all peer talk in classrooms is directly related to planned-for learning. For example, Janet Maybin's (2006) work provides evidence of rich meaning-making and identity-building among peers in informal interactions within the school setting.

Peer discussion is closely related to the broader concept of co-operative learning, in which pupils work together on academic tasks. While this is largely beyond the scope of this book, the nature of peer group organisation does have relevance. Alexander (2017, p 14) is among those who have noted in UK classrooms: *'the seeming paradox of children working everywhere in groups but rarely as groups'*. Considering contexts for dialogue in peer groups as a tool for learning, Cazden (2001) suggests that pupils commonly take on four intellectual roles in pair or small group activities, as shown in Table 5a.

Table 5a Intellectual roles in peer group work (adapted from Cazden, 2001)

Spontaneous helping	Pupils sharing informal requests and offers of help in the course of everyday classroom activities
Assigned teaching or tutoring	Pupils being empowered as experts in order to tutor peers on a specific, pre-learned topic
Reciprocal critique	Pupils providing constructive feedback to one another on ongoing work
Collaborative problem-solving	Pupils collaborating on a task often based on articulated social norms, sharing of ideas and challenge of others' ideas

Each of these roles is likely to result in a particular kind of talk with implications for the way in which the conditions for this are created. Spontaneous helping implies informal, unstructured interaction; assigned tutoring and reciprocal critique may be highly structured, bounded roles; collaborative problem-solving may be more open and highly complex in both social and cognitive terms. In the sections to follow, you will find out more about the most productive forms of peer talk and how to promote them.

5.3 What kinds of peer talk are there?

Categorising talk

Looking more closely at peer–peer talk, attempts have been made, through close scrutiny of transcripts, to categorise commonly occurring talk. One of the most influential typologies arose from detailed classroom research on 8–11 year-olds carried out in the 1990s. This led to a three-part model of how peers in a classroom commonly interact (Mercer and Littleton, 2007) summarised in Table 5b.

Table 5b Three ways of talking and thinking (adapted from Mercer and Littleton, 2007)

	Hallmarks	Verbal features
Disputational talk	Disagreement and individualised decision-making; little constructive criticism or pooling of resources	Short exchanges based on assertions and challenges
Cumulative talk	Building positively but uncritically on others' contributions; construction of common knowledge	Repetitions, confirmations, elaborations
Exploratory talk	Critical and constructive engagement with ideas; joint consideration of ideas; active participation from all	Justifications and alternatives offered; opinions sought; explicit reasoning

This framework has an evaluative dimension, as it implies that not all forms of peer talk are equally valuable. Disputational and cumulative talk are, in different ways, likely to be unproductive as vehicles for thinking, while exploratory talk, discussed in the next section, offers rich potential for co-constructing understanding. Other typologies of peer talk (eg Keefer et al, 2000), similarly distinguish between disagreement, consensus and more productive considerations of different viewpoints. Considering cumulative talk specifically, two things are striking. One is the issue of terminology. As seen in Section 4.4, cumulative talk – as an outcome of collective thinking – is a cornerstone of Alexander's (2017) vision of the dialogic classroom, but the term is used somewhat differently here to refer to an uncritical acceptance of others' views. The other is that harmony and early consensus are not necessarily desirable. Productive thinking in groups depends on subjecting ideas to robust challenge and the consideration of alternative perspectives.

Before turning to exploratory talk in more detail, it is important to note that Mercer and Littleton (2007) are clear that this model centres on academically productive peer talk and makes no attempt to analyse other social or affective functions. This is taken up in some ways by Maybin's (2006) ethnographic work on 10–12 year-old pupils. She identifies both 'duets' among friends, in which peers' contributions overlap and become almost indistinguishable, and 'conflictual talk', in which peers compete for the conversational floor. While these forms have echoes of cumulative and disputational talk respectively, they perhaps underline the fact that exploratory talk is much less likely to occur spontaneously. Nevertheless, fairly unstructured collaborative dialogue between friends may still be highly productive. Indeed, Vass et al (2014) argue that reasoning has been over-emphasised in evaluations of peer talk. They draw on transcripts from paired creative writing work to show how emotion-based connectivity leads to rich interaction through moments of, for example, humour, exuberance, shared frames of reference and enjoyment of content and process.

Exploratory talk

Exploratory talk, then, is a form of dialogue with particular potential for learning. Mercer (2000, p 98) defines it as:

That [form of talk] in which partners engage critically but constructively with each other's ideas. Relevant information is offered for joint consideration. Proposals may be challenged and counter-challenged, but if so reasons are given and alternatives are offered. Agreement is sought as a basis for joint progress. Knowledge is made publicly accountable and reasoning is visible in the talk.

Mercer and Littleton (2007, p 66) refer to this as: *'a distinctive social mode of thinking'*, thereby emphasising its role as a collective thought process. While exploratory talk is usually associated with peer interaction, you may notice some of the hallmarks of accountable talk introduced in Chapter 3 (Michaels et al, 2008) and also of the wider dialogic stance discussed at whole-class level in Chapter 4 (Wells and Arauz, 2006).

Although popularised as part of the model discussed at the start of this section, the concept of exploratory talk is also commonly identified with the earlier work of Douglas Barnes. Barnes (1976; 2008) draws attention to the tentative, hypothetical tone of this mode of peer-oriented talk, contrasting it with 'final draft', or 'presentational' speech, presented publicly for a teacher's approval (and valuable in its own right as a strand of oracy). Unlike presentational talk, exploratory talk is provisional and potentially cognitively liberating if teachers allow it time and space. The question of audience is a critical one, since Barnes suggests that formulating explanations and arguments for a listener who does not already know the answers is much more powerful than presenting to a teacher who has the authority of presumed expertise. This idea, of habitually being required to explain, links to a recent meta-analysis of 64 studies on self-explanation (Bisra et al, 2018). This long-established principle, found to be a powerful learning strategy, involves prompting pupils to explain a concept they are studying. Although, in this case, the explanation is not shared with others, the process of having to formulate an explanation, even hypothetically for another, has some parallels with the reasoning used in exploratory talk and has implications for the use of peer talk in classrooms.

5.4 How do learners make sense together through peer talk?

The workings of exploratory talk have been further explored in a variety of ways. Fernández et al (2015), based on studies of groups of pupils in the UK and Mexico, argue that, through exploratory talk, peers can exhibit as a group all of the features of a scaffolding role usually attributed to an adult or more knowledgeable other in 'asymmetrical' talk. Unpacking this mutual scaffolding further, Littleton and Mercer (2013) identify three process at work in what they term 'interthinking':

1. appropriation – learning strategies from peers that can then be applied independently;

2. co-construction – creating new ideas and strategies through collective reasoning that surpasses an individual's capabilities;

3. transformation – developing transferable metacognitive understanding about individual reasoning.

The last of these, they argue, is particularly powerful because it concerns the impact of social experience on subsequent individual cognition.

A number of researchers have attempted to explore in detail the specific mechanisms of this process of collective sense-making. Barnes and Todd (1977) identify four categories of 'collaborative move' associated with productive learning:

1. initiating – introducing a new topic;

2. eliciting – inviting contributions from others;

3. extending – building on one another's ideas;

4. qualifying – airing complexities, limitations and contradictions.

In addition to talking about the content of the learning, exploratory talk may also feature utterances which serve to regulate the discourse process itself. Gillies (2016) expands on this idea of *teachable* strategies. She draws on extracts from science enquiry work from pupils trained in dialogic strategies to identify – alongside non-verbal strategies such as open body language and encouraging sounds – the verbal strategies seen in Table 5c.

Table 5c Verbal strategies to teach pupils

Strategy to be taught (Gillies, 2016)	Example opener
Asking open questions	*'How might we...?'*
Paraphrasing or re-voicing key ideas	*'So what you are suggesting is...'*
Summarising the main points of a process	*'So far we've found out that...'*
Using empathic listening skills	*'It sounds like you found it hard to...'*
Clarifying misperceptions	*'I'm not sure what you mean by....'*
Assertively expressing a point of view	*'I see what you mean but instead we could try...'*
Offering suggestions tentatively	*'Would it be worth considering this as a plan...?*
Offering self-disclosure	*'When that happened to me, I felt...'*

The following case study shows an instance of exploratory talk in a Year 8 classroom.

Case study

History classroom: exploratory talk extract

Pupils have been given the task of matching and then sequencing pictures and captions relating to the slave trade. One stage of the 'triangle of trade' is missing and must be added and explained.

Ben	What does this say? Captured and taken to the coast.
Nathan	Where does it go then?
Ben	It goes with this, so that's the first one I think.
Kiran	Wait, how about we put all the captions with pictures first?
Nathan	Yeah, then we'll see...so, wait, I can see already what the missing one is. It's where they sell the slaves in England. That – what do you call it?
Kiran	Auction. Yeah but...
Ben	Yeah, the auction where they choose the best ones.
Nathan	No, wait, they don't get sold in England, do they?
Ben	Yeah, it was places like Liverpool, remember?
Kiran	No it started there, but the slaves were working in the West Indies at the end weren't they? So that's where they sold them.
Nathan	So, hang on...the boat started in Liverpool but not with slaves?
Ben	Where do the slaves come in? We've got this picture where they're on the big ship – the one with them all crowded in.
Nathan	Oh yes, they were in Africa first. That's where they were captured. Is that what you mean, Ben?
Kiran	Yeah, they came from Africa but got sold in those places like Jamaica. We all need to agree this, so are we agreeing now? This is where they are captured, this is on the boat and this is in the fields?
Ben	So we are saying the auction is the missing one and it goes here?
Nathan	Yeah, the auction, definitely. And what do we need to say about that?

What can be seen in this brief extract is a hint of the tentative dialogue characteristic of exploratory talk, as the exchange builds towards a purposeful outcome. There are some collaborative moves as, for example, Ben builds on Nathan's understanding of an auction and Nathan elicits more detail from Kiran about the capture of the slaves. There is also some evidence of meta-talk in Kiran's attempts to keep the task on track with strategies like matching pictures with captions, summarising and seeking consensus. What these pupils would benefit from now is a greater focus on extending and qualifying ideas.

5.5 What evidence is there for the benefits of peer talk?

Fostering productive talk in group situations can be complex. It is reasonable, therefore, to consider what evidence exists for benefits arising from high-quality peer discussion, particularly as monitoring groups for productive talk has been deemed an under-researched area (Howe, 2014; Reznitskaya et al, 2009). In this section, the evidence arising from three specific programmes centred on this form of pedagogy is considered.

Mercer and Littleton (2007) offer a variety of findings related to the use of exploratory talk using the Thinking Together approach, which has resulted in a range of teaching materials for various age groups. Thinking Together is a programme based on establishing ground rules and delivering carefully structured group discussion lessons. The independent group work component, centred on specific activity stimuli provided, is framed by teacher-led whole-class introductions and concluding plenary discussions and the materials have subsequently been published as teacher guides (eg Dawes et al, 2004). Mercer and Littleton (2007) report on four main studies over a number of years, on pupils between the ages of 6 and 14, comparing intervention to control groups. Following participation in Thinking Together lessons, they show, for example, increased attainment in English assessments for Year 8 pupils and improved performance in science, mathematics and reasoning tests for Year 5 pupils. This UK team has also collaborated with colleagues in Mexico. Through similar interventions, improved performance among Mexican pupils has been found on reasoning tests (Rojas-Drummond and Mercer, 2003) and reading comprehension assessments (Rojas-Drummond et al, 2014), showing the potential for this approach to transcend cultures.

Looking beyond the specific Thinking Together materials, exploratory talk has also been evaluated in South African secondary science classrooms through a similar process of teacher professional development and lessons based on discussion-rich activities. Webb et al (2017) report on a number of studies carried out in this context, based on a rigorous experimental design. A consistent finding was that the exploratory talk in science led to transferable gains, beyond science itself, in reasoning tests. This is seen as significant, as it is an example of 'far transfer', or the application of learning to a new task, different in either content or context from where the original learning took place (Barnett and Ceci, 2002). Webb at al (2017) speculate that this transfer may be due to features of exploratory talk that are consistent with current knowledge about learning science, such as learning dialogue routines that help to manage working memory capacity.

While exploratory talk is often associated with independent interaction among peers, other programmes fit more closely with Alexander's (2017) category of teacher-led collective group work. Researchers in the US have developed an approach known as Collaborative Reasoning (Clark et al, 2003), which shares many features with Philosophy for Children (Lipman, 1998), a programme which will be discussed in depth in Chapter 6. Collaborative Reasoning is based on a seven-step process whereby pupils discuss a provocative question, sometimes involving a moral dilemma, arising from their reading of a story. They explain and elaborate on their views, challenge others' ideas and finally vote and review the discussion. Apart from providing the initial stimulus, the teacher has only a facilitating role and pupils are free to make reasoned contributions, openly building on one another's ideas (Reznitskaya et al, 2009).

Collaborative Reasoning has been extensively researched. Sun et al (2015) summarise a number of studies showing the development of argument skills and problem-solving strategies, which were found to transfer to new contexts, while the meta-analysis of discussion-based comprehension activities by Murphy et al (2009), points towards gains in not only basic comprehension, but high-level critical thinking. Reznitskaya et al's (2009) findings include improved individual performance transferring to subsequent reflective writing tasks among Grade 4 and 5 pupils. The basis of this transfer of learning is the principle that pupils are developing through this structured process a schema for argumentation, through which they internalise this form of discourse, much like Mercer and Littleton's explanation of transformation through exploratory talk. While Collaborative Reasoning, like Thinking Together, centres on peer dialogue, regulated to a great extent by pupils themselves, Gillies (2016) highlights the subtle but important role of the teacher, eliciting elaboration, challenge and review.

A further example of peer talk involving some initial teacher facilitation is Reciprocal Teaching (Palinscar and Brown, 1984). In this case, the object is to improve pupils' comprehension of texts. Stimulated, to begin with, by teacher modelling, pupils learn to regulate their own discussion through activities which make explicit the process of successful reading for understanding: summarising, questioning, clarifying and predicting. As the children grow in confidence, the teacher increasingly withdraws and responsibility is transferred to the pupils, who take turns as the 'dialogue leader'. Palinscar and Brown's (1984) own initial studies, mainly involving US Grade 7 pupils, found that the Reciprocal Teaching intervention led to improvements, beyond those of the control groups, not only in the quality of dialogue itself but in comprehension test scores. These benefits were found within naturalistic classroom environments and were sustained over time.

Since then, Reciprocal Teaching has been widely evaluated. Hattie (2012), based on meta-analysis of 38 studies, reports an effect size of 0.74 for this approach, well above the average of 0.40 and the highest of all the teaching strategies investigated. Gillies (2016) summarises a number of studies from the last 20 years that report similar, convincing gains in attainment on comprehension tests, albeit also reflecting some of the challenges involved, such as the high degree of scaffolding sometimes needed. Another interesting caveat is offered by McKeown and Beck (2015). They acknowledge the impact on comprehension of what they broadly term 'strategies' approaches, including Reciprocal Teaching. However, they also note that this can lead to dialogue that is heavily focused on process and the enactment of routines, but lacking deep engagement with the actual meaning and content of the text. The implication may therefore be that the most powerful impact lies in the transferable benefits, such as argumentation schema (Reznitskaya et al, 2009) encountered earlier. This echoes Littleton and Mercer's (2013) idea of individual transformation through interthinking, involving the internalisation of externally introduced routines, in line with the Vygotskian ideas introduced in Chapter 2.

5.6 How can productive peer talk be promoted?

Productive group dialogue depends on a variety of factors and is far from straightforward. Littleton and Mercer (2013), for example, suggest that learners using exploratory talk need to:

- freely offer constructive criticism;
- receive constructive criticism;
- treat and scrutinise ideas from all with equal respect;
- share relevant information with the group;
- justify proposals;
- seek relevant information from peers;
- check for agreement on proposals;
- reflect on the discussion process.

The next sections explore what is known about creating the conditions for this to flourish. While there is an extensive literature around group work and co-operative learning in a wider sense, the focus here is on those aspects germane to productive discussion.

Structuring peer discussion: the group

In their seminal work on small group communication, Barnes and Todd (1977) identify group composition as a central consideration. While there is consensus on the importance of this, views on the details differ somewhat. One aspect of this is the size of group which Blatchford et al (2003), reviewing group work literature, suggest is an under-researched issue. Some researchers have suggested a maximum of four members (Barnes and Todd; 1977; Gillies, 2016). This is consistent with the work of the Social Pedagogic Research into Group Work (SPRinG) project with learners aged 5–14 (Baines et al, 2009), which also stipulated, and saw success with, groups of four. However, while SPRinG was an extensive, multi-year intervention involving teacher development and classroom materials, its aim was to develop learning in groups more generally, rather than directly promoting talk itself. With the aim of generating exploratory talk more specifically, the Thinking Together materials (Dawes et al, 2004) recommend groups of three, to avoid a split into two pairs.

Exploratory talk is also influenced by the combination of learners. There is general agreement that good relationships are fundamental in group work (Baines et al, 2008; Blatchford et al, 2003), but while some have stressed the importance of working in a group in which a child feels comfortable (Barnes and Todd, 1977), the teams researching exploratory talk explicitly argue against friendship groups (Mercer and Littleton, 2007). This is based on the need to consider diverse perspectives and avoid uncritical early consensus. In terms of the optimum mix of abilities within a group (recognising that 'ability' implies an unhelpfully fixed view of potential), there is much less agreement. Nevertheless, focusing specifically on the talk generated, research by Schmitz and Winskel (2008) on different pairs in Australian Year 6 mathematics lessons found that exploratory talk is more likely in relatively 'symmetrical' pairings, which avoid extremes of ability. Similarly, while stability of groupings is often advocated in terms of general productive group working (Baines et al, 2015; Blatchford et al, 2003), for the purposes of exploratory talk, Mercer and Littleton (2007) suggest children working with a range of partners. These distinctions – between group work outcomes generally and exploratory talk specifically – reinforce the special status of exploratory talk as tentative and hypothetical. While consensus is sought eventually, efficient problem-solving is not the chief aim and the process may involve hesitations and digressions or, as Barnes (1976, p 28) put it, *groping towards a meaning*.

Structuring peer discussion: ground rules

In order to develop these good working relationships among peers, some attention has been given to the development of ground rules for talking in groups. This is based on an acknowledgement that successful talk requires children to be taught how to interact appropriately (Gillies, 2016). Littleton and Mercer (2013) point out that patterns of interaction in any social setting are governed by a distinctive set of norms. In everyday life, these conventions may be only tacitly agreed but, in the classroom, such ground rules can be made explicit. In an echo of the hallmarks of exploratory talk listed in Section 5.6, Mercer and Dawes (2008) propose a generic list of ground rules centred on principles of participation, reasoning, challenge of ideas and joint decision-making. Importantly, however, the approach to exploratory talk seen in the Thinking Together materials involves co-constructing ground rules with children and then using them as a common reference point for reflecting on the process of talk (Mercer and Littleton, 2007). Collaborative Reasoning also features ground rules, such as not talking over others, looking at both sides of an issue and responding to the idea rather than the person (Clark et al, 2003). However, in this case, these guidelines are pre-determined rather than negotiated, reflecting the more structured, process-driven nature of this form of peer talk.

Structuring peer discussion: the task

The task itself also needs careful consideration if it is to promote talk. Gillies (2016) reviews a number of studies and identifies features of particularly productive tasks. Such tasks are likely, for example, to be: open, challenging, complex, problem-based, ill-structured and lacking obvious procedures and outcomes. As Gillies points out, pupils have much to gain when working together on problems like this. In line with this need to provide a task with a *reason* to talk together, Mercer et al (2017a), based on their exploratory talk research, propose four conditions:

1. all participants must need to talk in order to complete the task;

2. activity should encourage co-operation, rather than competition;

3. participants need a shared understanding of the activity's purpose;

4. participants need some awareness of how to use talk in this way.

A key point here is perhaps the first: the explicit need for talk as an integral component of the task. In this vein, Barnes and Todd (1977) emphasises that teachers need to make clear to learners that they are specifically seeking different perspectives on an issue and that this process of collective thinking is valued alongside – or even above – any end product. Howe (2014) reinforces this idea: reflecting on a range of her previous studies in science spanning ages from eight to adult, she concludes that progress towards conceptual mastery within group tasks hinges on discussing contrasting ideas and that this is the biggest predictor of knowledge gain (Howe, 2014). Similarly, Webb et al's (2014) study of primary pupils' mathematical problem-solving found that the biggest predictor of achievement was the level of engagement with, and building on, other pupils' ideas, whether in agreement or not. This accords with the ideas of cognitive conflict encountered in Chapter 2, of course, but how this mutual engagement is achieved depends to a great extent on the teacher, who retains an important role.

Structuring peer discussion: the teacher's role

In considering the role of the teacher, a variety of positions have been proposed. Some of the forms of peer discussion previously mentioned incorporate a designated role for the teacher. For example, Reciprocal Teaching requires the teacher to model the four comprehension activities before gradually ceding ownership to pupils (Palinscar and Brown, 1984), while Collaborative Reasoning involves the teacher being specifically trained in a process of facilitation (Clark et al, 2003), which may involve regular interjections. In contrast, during tasks aiming to generate exploratory talk, as enacted through Thinking Together lessons, the teacher's role is much less overt. In these lessons, the emphasis is instead on the teacher's *preparatory* work. The teacher's job is to create a suitable context, model exploratory talk with the whole class before and after group work and rehearse the ground rules (Mercer and Littleton, 2007). While Mercer and Littleton acknowledge the need for timely interventions in group discussions, the teacher is not primarily positioned as a participant.

In between these two positions lies an interesting middle ground of responsive, contingent teacher responses. Gillies (2016) draws on her many studies of group discussions to show the positive impact on the quality of discussion, but also reasoning and problem-solving, when teachers are trained in specific linguistic tools to enhance the talk. She also finds that pupils subsequently adopt for themselves the discourse modelled by the teacher. In one particular study, Gillies and Boyle (2008, p 1337) closely examine what they term the *mediated-learning behaviours* of some of the teachers who had undergone such training, as shown in Table 5d. You may notice that these resemble the enquiry questions at whole-class level introduced in Chapter 3.

Table 5d Teachers' mediated-learning behaviours for groups

Teacher behaviour (Gillies and Boyle, 2008)	Examples of a teacher's verbal interventions
Challenging questions	Probing further: *'What was…?'*
Cognitive questions	Asking for reasons: *'Tell us why…'*
Metacognitive questions	Thinking about thinking: *'What do we know so far?'*
Prompts	Moving discussion on: *'What could you consider next?'*
Focus on issues	Zooming in: *'Let's look at…specifically.'*
Open questions	Eliciting more information: *'Tell us more about…'*
Validation and acknowledgement of efforts	Noting specific achievements: *'It's great to see how you've worked well today on…'*

Looking more closely, Newman (2017) provides a detailed analysis of one teacher's interventions and draws attention to the skilled switching of modes. In an echo of the different communicative approaches (Mortimer and Scott, 2003) encountered in Chapter 4, Newman shows how, in the process of scaffolding and modelling group dialogue, a teacher may move between transmissive and exploratory contributions and between authoritative and informal tones. In addition to these examples, Webb et al (2014), reporting on US primary pupils' mathematical problem-solving, draw particular attention to the power of teacher follow-up comments and questions which prompt pupils to engage with others' ideas and to relate and compare their own ideas. The teacher's role in modelling these 'expanded responses' that draw in and build on prior contributions has also been found by Rajala et al (2012) to be crucial in ensuring inclusive, 'symmetrical' forms of group discussion. The common thread across these positions is the teacher's strategic and skilled role in creating and maintaining the conditions for talk.

Case study

Embedding the ground rules

Conor was keen to develop peer talk with his Year 1 class of 5–6 year-olds. A lesson on freezing and melting provided an opportunity for collaborative problem-solving and Conor approached the introduction of ground rules as an ongoing process extending beyond this lesson itself, as seen in the example below.

Table 5e Working with ground rules

Providing a suitable stimulus	Conor knew that an intriguing problem without a single solution was needed to provoke productive talk. Building on images of the real life discovery of frozen mammoths preserved in ice, small toy dinosaurs had been frozen in small pots and then turned out. The children had to plan how to release the dinosaurs from the ice without causing damage.
Modelling the issues	Conor and his teaching assistant modelled a discussion in which there were frequent interruptions, unco-operative behaviour and ultimately a failure to listen to one another. The children were invited to comment on what had gone wrong.
Agreeing the ground rules	The children were then asked to come up with suggestions for how this discussion could have been handled better. Conor re-voiced where necessary and his teaching assistant scribed the ideas in a list, including things like: taking turns, letting everyone have a say and using 'kind voices'. The children were now ready to talk in groups of three.
Noticing the ground rules in action	As the planning discussions began, Conor circulated, listening for examples of good talking, noting down children's specific phrases and talk moves. Stopping the class, he was then able to share what he had noticed, drawing attention to salient features: *'It was great to hear Jay saying: "Have you thought about how to hold the ice while it melts?" That gives his group a good idea to think about.'*
Valuing the ground rules	The lesson concluded with a plenary discussion. As well as asking what had been learned about the subject content (melting and freezing), Conor asked what the children had learned about talking together and how useful their rules had been. This made clear to the children that the *process* of talking was valued alongside the end *product* of understanding scientific content.
Keeping the ground rules alive	Conor wanted to build on this early attempt in subsequent lessons. He had taken photographs of a few groups. He printed them for display, adding speech bubbles to reflect the appropriate talk moves he had witnessed. This provided a visual reference point for future lessons.

What this example illustrates is the way that ground rules can be reinforced before, during and after an activity, helping to create an ethos going beyond any one lesson.

5.7 What are the challenges associated with peer talk?

The complexity of planning for productive peer talk will already be apparent from the discussion in Section 5.6. Howe and Abedin's (2013) systematic review of classroom dialogue studies notes that teachers find exploratory talk extremely difficult to promote. A number of challenges are identified from this body of research, including the need to educate pupils in the purpose and procedures of dialogue and the delicate balance required between exploring diverse views and ensuring curriculum coverage. The second of these points highlights the use of teachers' judgment to identify the moments best suited to a more open exploration of ideas. While renowned as a proponent of exploratory talk, Barnes (2008) nevertheless supports this view that carefully orchestrated group discussion is just one of many forms of classroom communication: *'it is a valuable resource in a teacher's repertoire but it is not a universal remedy'* (p 7).

The case for using peer collaboration and dialogue judiciously is reinforced by the cognitive science insights mentioned in the previous chapter and their warnings about the additional 'cognitive load' demands of minimally guided approaches to learning (Kirschner et al, 2006). Hattie's (2009) extensive meta-analysis of studies reinforces this point by contrasting interventions involving the teacher as an *activator* with those in which the teacher is a *facilitator*. Overall effect sizes for interventions in which the teacher plays an active role (eg setting clear goals and providing responsive feedback) are far higher than for those based on a more passive stance. This does not, however, preclude a high-profile role for peer discussion – indeed, Hattie's highest-rated example of a teacher-activated intervention is Reciprocal Teaching – but it suggests that, along with the role of the teacher, its structure and its position in a sequence of learning are paramount.

Cognitive science has been applied more specifically to peer interaction by Kirschner et al (2018), who suggest implications for the design of such activities in order to ensure that the potential advantages of harnessing a group's *collective* working memory outweigh the additional cognitive burden of managing the collaboration itself. Kirschner et al suggest that making collaboration effective depends on:

- sufficiently complex tasks that make collaboration worthwhile;
- clear guidance and support for collaboration;
- a small group with clearly defined roles;

- group members with expertise in the subject matter at a similar level;

- good collaborative skills and prior experience of working together.

You will notice that these principles, based on cognitive science, bear out those arising from other forms of research, as cited in Section 5.6, and that the very notion of collective working memory has echoes of interthinking, introduced in Chapter 2 (Littleton and Mercer, 2013).

5.8 Summary

Children talk to their peers in a variety of contexts within the classroom but not all forms of discussion are productive. Exploratory talk is a form of dialogue with particular potential for learning. It involves the co-construction of meaning through a process of reasoning and challenge, featuring a number of identifiable and teachable talk moves. Exploratory talk, which may be known under a variety of names, has been shown to benefit pupils' reasoning but also transferable performance in subject assessments. Productive peer talk depends on attention to group composition, ground rules, appropriate tasks and the flexible, responsive role of the teacher. Among the challenges involved are the need to decide when and how to incorporate peer collaboration discussion as part of a wider repertoire of classroom activity.

- Which learning experiences in your classroom might be most suitable for promoting peer dialogue?

- How could you design an activity, or adapt an existing one, in order to require pupils to speak and share their ideas?

- What ground rules would your class need in order to be able to engage in productive dialogue?

Exploring further

The University of Cambridge team associated with Neil Mercer and colleagues, as encountered in this chapter, have useful resources for promoting exploratory talk:

- https://oracycambridge.org/resources (accessed 17 May 2019).

The Thinking Together project site also has useful teaching resources:

- https://thinkingtogether.educ.cam.ac.uk/resources (accessed 17 May 2019).

This book covers many of the principles of exploratory talk and 'interthinking' more broadly:

- Littleton, K and Mercer, N (2013) *Interthinking: Putting Talk to Work*. Abingdon: Routledge.

Chapter 6
Classroom talk and the twenty-first century learner

6.1 Chapter overview

This chapter will outline:

6.2   what is meant by learning for the twenty-first century;

6.3   how classroom talk relates to technology;

6.4   how classroom talk relates to self-regulated learning and metacognition;

6.5   how classroom talk relates to critical thinking.

6.2 How does classroom talk relate to ideas about twenty-first century learning?

The increasing globalisation of education noted in Chapter 1 and consequent 'policy-borrowing' has fuelled long-standing debates about the purpose of schooling and what is to be taught. For some, this has led to an emphasis on knowledge-rich curricula and substantive content in an attempt to emulate the attainment levels of high-performing nations or to promote social mobility (Hirsch, 2009; Young, 2013). Others have argued for a response based on developing transferable, lifelong skills and dispositions needed for the workplaces of the future (Claxton, 2008; Ritchhart, 2015). Whether any of this is truly new, or uniquely tied to the twenty-first century, is debatable, of course, as is setting up these positions as a dichotomy between knowledge and skills. The two are intertwined: knowledge often becomes understanding through its application in novel ways, while skill development requires some substantive content with which to work.

From this more integrated perspective, the OECD (2018) have begun to develop a global learning framework for preparing pupils to thrive in an uncertain future. This involves *'the mobilisation of knowledge, skills, attitudes and values to meet complex demands'* (OECD, 2018, p 5). Among the skills through which they envisage knowledge will be applied are collaboration – at the heart of much of this book – but also critical thinking, self-regulation and the use of technology. It is important to be clear that identifying these skills as significant is not to argue for them being taught discretely, or even necessarily in generic, transferable terms. Indeed, evidence from cognitive science suggests that the academic content comprising much of schooling ('biologically secondary knowledge') is highly domain-specific (Sweller, 2016) and that skills like critical thinking are also embedded in content (Willingham, 2007). On that basis, this chapter seeks to explore briefly the relationship and contribution of classroom talk to these aspects of the framework.

6.3 How does classroom talk relate to technology?

Perspectives on talk and technology

Cazden (2001) proposes four ways in which technology might intersect with classroom talk:

1. talk *with* computers: pupils interacting with computers;

2. talk *at* computers: pupils interacting with one another at a computer;

3. talk *through* computers: pupils using technology to interact at a distance;

4. talk *in relation to* computers: pupils using talk away from the computer for broader activities in which technology plays a role.

While this remains a useful conceptual map, much has changed since 2001, with technology now playing at least some role in most activities pupils encounter. A recent review of themes emerging from the research on dialogue and technology identifies three ways in which digital technology has been found to enhance dialogue (Major et al, 2018), as shown in Table 6a.

Teachers will need to judge which of these contributions could equally well be achieved without technology and which of them – particularly in the technological affordances category – offer something distinctly different. Indeed, it could be argued, based on the examples to follow, that there is little evidence of technology, for all its advantages, having a unique and irreplaceable impact on talk.

Table 6a Technology enhancing dialogue (adapted from Major et al, 2018)

Dialogue activity	• Exposure to alternative perspectives
	• Co-construction of understanding (eg collaborating on, or sharing, a digital artefact)
	• Expressions of metacognitive learning (eg reflecting on own or others' thinking)
	• Scaffolding others' understanding (pupil to pupil and teacher–pupil)
Technological affordances	• Creation of a shared dialogic space
	• Mediating interaction (eg sharing content)
	• Externalisation of ideas (eg making misconceptions visible)
	• Multimodal delivery of content
	• Allowing ideas to be adapted and changed
	• Recording and revisiting of ideas (eg sustaining thinking across lessons)
Learning environment	• Learner autonomy
	• Inclusion of learners
	• Improved sense of community
	• Improved interpersonal relationships
	• Learner motivation and engagement

Talking with and at computers: technology as a stimulus for talk

Wegerif and Dawes (2004) identify the computer's potential for promoting a new type of interaction. In contrast to a version of the limited IRF pattern discussed in Chapter 3, their important insight from research is that software can provide an opportunity for an IDRF exchange. The 'D' denotes a *discussion* phase, in which pupils sit back from the computer and consider their response. This signifies a new relationship with the computer, in which pupils appear to be in control during the discussion activity. In this sense, IDRF also represents a bridge between Cazden's (2001) talk *with* and talk *at* categories: pupils are interacting with the computer but also with one another. Wegerif (2007) suggests that this represents a computer-supported ZPD. While such a discussion phase could of course be incorporated into a traditional teacher-led exchange, Mercer and Littleton (2007) suggest that the added value of the computer here is its ambivalent and patient contribution. This contrasts with the fast-paced, exposing and competitive environment that can be a feature of traditional whole-class recitation episodes.

The dialogic space created by the computer's role is also a feature of research on the role of the interactive whiteboard (IWB). Various studies have explored the IWB as a tool for creating a dialogic space, which *'opens up when two or more perspectives are held in tension'* (Wegerif, 2007, p 4). Hennessy's (2011) studies of teacher-led IWB use in mainly secondary classrooms, suggest its potential both for teachers eliciting contrasting ideas and for allowing learners to construct and work on digital artefacts jointly. The focus on pupils', rather than teachers', use of the IWB is the subject of research in primary science lessons on categorisation tasks. This suggests that features of exploratory talk can be generated through IWB-based activities which allow for externalisation of thinking and modification of ideas (Kershner et al, 2010; Mercer et al, 2017a). As pointed out by Littleton and Mercer (2013), in the context of primary science, it is the ease of provisional recording and amendment of ideas which is especially productive. They characterise such examples as improvable objects which offer a *'halfway stage between the ephemerality of talk and the permanence of written texts'* (Littleton and Mercer, 2013, p 77). The same process of externalising and capturing otherwise fleeting collaborative talk has also been achieved through the use of software enabling pupils to voice their ideas through on-screen characters (Wegerif, 2007). In this case, the software was Bubble Dialogue but there are now many online tools to create similar effects, as shown at the end of this chapter.

A further example of technology as a stimulus for talk is provided by Collins and White (2015). Building on the idea of accountable talk (Michaels et al, 2008) introduced here in Chapter 3, they report on the creation of an online environment providing prompts for different roles, such the evidence manager, within a group. As well as improvements in generic enquiry skills, pupils were found to have internalised and understood the various metacognitive strategies taught, a theme that is developed in Section 6.4.

Talking through and at computers: technology as an environment for talk

Taking another perspective on the creation of dialogic space, there is a strand of research examining Computer-Mediated Communication (CMC) as a form of dialogue. Asterhan (2015) identifies various advantages of online dialogue at a distance, including being able to keep track of contributions, improved participation and reduced inhibition. Others, however, identify potential limitations such as 'communicative anxiety' caused by the lack of non-verbal cues and immediate responses (Wegerif, 2007) and the way that, while today's pupils may be very familiar with this *mode* of interaction, they may not share with their teachers the same understanding of the appropriate *genre* of communication when using technology (Kleine Staarman, 2009). As Mercer and Littleton (2013) point out, the need for agreed ground rules, albeit possibly different ones from face-to-face contexts, remains.

While online dialogue is of relevance in as far as it exhibits many of the features of peer talk identified in Chapter 5, the focus of this book is firmly on spoken language. To this end, two forms of CMC may be of particular interest. Firstly, Asterhan (2015) reports studies cautiously suggesting that skills developed in online environments might transfer to face-to-face contexts. In one of these, Iordanou (2013) worked with sixth-grade pupils debating scientific and social issues via online instant messaging and found that argument skills subsequently improved in spoken activities compared with control groups. This improvement is attributed in part to a reduction in complexity since, in the electronic environment, argument is not complicated by verbal and social demands. Other powerful examples of CMC blend talking *through* and *at* computers. Wegerif (2007) describes classroom work using the Philosophy for Children approach found in Section 6.5. The in-class discussions generated outcomes which were shared via online forums with schools in other countries. In a similar vein, Cook et al (2019) analyse transcripts of talk within secondary geography lessons. These lessons involved a microblogging tool as a means of sharing ideas between different groups within the classroom. This allowed pupils to interact through the computer but then with their peers face-to-face, as they considered other groups' contributions, thereby providing examples of all three of Major et al's (2018) categories: dialogue activity, technological affordances and the creation of a new learning environment.

Embedding technology effectively

While technology has potential, therefore, for promoting classroom talk, a scoping review by Major et al (2018) also highlights many challenges from the research in this area. Challenges for pupils include a lack of technical skills, unhelpful expectations of technology and distraction or frustration arising from this medium. Challenges for teachers also involve technical skills, as well as a lack of appropriate resources, the need to foster effective collaboration and a wide range of pedagogical and managerial issues. The authors note that many of these challenges are interconnected and often actually centre on generic issues associated with implementing a dialogic pedagogy. This shift away from a view of technology as something discrete links to the approach taken in the Thinking Together lessons discussed in Chapter 5. Computer-based work, in this model, is set within the broader context of collective thinking activities, so that: '*It is the pedagogy that is paramount, not the technology*' (Mercer et al, 2017a, p 11).

The point here is that learning the strategies for effective collaboration and talk away from the computer first leads to much more productive work at the computer. Rather than conceptualising computer-based learning as located in the software, Mercer and Littleton (2007) see it as one embedded component in a wider relationship involving learners, teacher and activities. This underlines the argument for a reciprocal relationship: as well as technology enhancing talk, the development of effective spoken communication strategies enables a far more productive use of technology. When internalised, these strategies are a form of self-regulation, which is the subject of the next section.

6.4 How does classroom talk relate to self-regulated learning and metacognition?

What is self-regulated learning and metacognition and why it is important?

Zimmerman (2002, p 65) defines self-regulation as *'the self-directive process by which learners transform their mental abilities into academic skills'* and suggests this involves cyclical phases of forethought, performance and self-reflection. The EEF (2018b) suggests that such self-regulated learning has three components.

1. Cognition: the mental process of knowing, understanding and learning.

2. Metacognition: the monitoring and directing of one's learning.

3. Motivation: the willingness to apply cognitive and metacognitive skills to one's learning.

At the heart of this is metacognition, a term sometimes used more or less synonymously with self-regulation and associated particularly with the 1970s work of John Flavell. Flavell (1979) draws attention to metacognitive knowledge, its application to metacognitive experiences and the enactment of this awareness through conscious metacognitive strategies directed towards specific metacognitive goals. Since Flavell's early work in this field, a wide range of evidence attests to the impact of cultivating this form of self-awareness. Perry et al (2018), in a systematic review of the literature relating to the teaching of metacognition, find strong evidence of a positive impact on pupil outcomes. This links to the EEF's (2018a) research summary, pointing towards this being a high-impact and low-cost intervention and with Hattie's (2012) meta-analysis suggesting large effect sizes for approaches related to metacognition. Hattie (2012), however, is clear that many of these strategies are rooted in subject matter and may not be easily transferable across content domains, while the EEF (2018a) similarly emphasises that the bulk of the evidence available is for subject-specific work, rather than generic thinking skills.

The role of talk in self-regulated learning and metacognition

In her review of literature on metacognition, Lai (2011) highlights studies showing the impact of collaborative or co-operative learning on metacognition and in a guidance report also drawing on a review of evidence, the EEF (2018b) identifies promoting and developing metacognitive talk as one of its seven key recommendations. In doing so, the EEF makes an explicit link to dialogic teaching. Alexander (2017) reinforces this, emphasising that dialogic teaching involves exploring thought processes as well as content. In line with this, as well as the repertoires of talk for teaching introduced in Chapter 4, Alexander (2017) also considers talk for *learning*. Learners, he suggests, should develop their own repertoire which includes modes such as: explaining, questioning, speculating, evaluating and negotiating – all of which are likely to enhance the monitoring and directing of learning associated with metacognition. This connection is noted by Reznitskaya and Gregory (2013, p 117), who describe dialogic enquiry as *'inherently metacognitive'*. They base this assertion on dialogic strategies such as:

- pupils learning to ask peers for clarification during discussion;
- teachers making learning purposeful by modelling and encouraging reasoning;
- pupils learning to evaluate different perspectives by considering open-ended questions;
- teachers and pupils making strengths and limitations of pupil reasoning visible to the whole group.

Looking beyond dialogic teaching specifically, you may have noticed that many other models of productive talk encountered in this book also have distinctly metacognitive features. Three of many possible examples are considered here.

1. Agreeing ground rules for exploratory talk among peers were discussed in Section 5.6 and Littleton and Mercer (2013) suggest that children's reference back to them aids the transfer of responsibility for co-regulation from the teacher to the group.

2. Explicit structure is also a feature of collaborative reasoning, introduced in Section 5.5. Reznitskaya et al (2009) show how experience with these scaffolded discussions leads to pupils internalising a schema for

argumentation. This includes specific language structures suitable for reasoning and arguing that can be applied in new situations.

3. The Cognitive Acceleration in Science Education approach explored in Section 4.6 (Adey and Shayer, 2015) has metacognition as one of its three 'pillars': each lesson features a teacher-prompted reflection not only on the learning gained collaboratively but on the learning process itself.

These metacognitive elements of talk are closely linked to benefits for assessment. Black and Wiliam's (1998a) seminal and extensive review of research literature draws attention to the need to involve pupils in their own learning through, for example, peer and self-assessment. Their subsequent work over two decades on a model of assessment for learning brings high quality dialogue to provoke reflection squarely into the foreground (Black and Wiliam, 1998b; 2018). This overlap, in which dialogic talk is viewed as a tool for assessment, as well as learning, has been noted by others and indeed, the term 'dialogic assessment' has been proposed as an alternative to 'assessment for learning' (Fisher, 2009; Alexander, 2017). As well as these incidental links, some research has set out to investigate more specifically the metacognitive elements of classroom talk and three recent studies offer valuable insights for teachers.

Evidence linking self-regulated learning and metacognition with talk

As seen in the examples cited in the previous section, collaborative activity may help not only to develop self-regulation, but also to promote forms of group co-regulation. Pino-Pasternak et al (2018) see interpersonal regulation as one of three dimensions – together with social dynamics and the nature of group dialogue – determining how productive peer collaboration is. Their study of Year 1 children's work on mathematics problem-solving suggests that children evaluated by their teacher as being highly self-regulated consistently adopted the pivotal roles within the group, either leading the task or scaffolding others. Children in the latter role used sophisticated language to achieve this. Evidence was also found of effective co-regulation, as responsibility for regulating the task shifted among the group. This implies that, even with these very young learners, the capacity to self- and co-regulate learning influences the quality of dialogue and the outcome of tasks, lending weight to arguments for these skills to be taught explicitly.

As well as the explicit teaching of metacognitive skills, Kuhn and Zillmer (2015) show how these might also be fostered through exposure to rich opportunities for dialogue. They report on a three-year intervention with US middle-school pupils based on structured debates and subsequent reflections on the dialogue. In an echo of one of the strategies discussed in Section 6.3, face-to-face talk in pairs was stimulated by electronic dialogue with other pairs representing different views. As well as talk about the subject matter, the researchers identified talk about the discourse itself, which they dub 'meta-talk'. The quality of argument improved in both the verbal exchanges and subsequent written work when compared with a non-intervention group. The types of meta-talk identified were:

- metacomprehension, relating to understanding statements made;
- meta-argument, relating to considering the merits of a specific argument;
- meta-argumentation, relating to the process of the argument.

Identifying and categorising these talk moves allows teachers to plan to teach them explicitly. Nevertheless, it is important to note that the development of meta-talk was the result of intense engagement and practice (Kuhn and Zillmer, 2015) and the powerful category of meta-argumentation, governing the norms of discourse, was particularly slow to develop.

The link between metacognitive talk and wider educational outcomes has been explored in the US by Zepeda et al (2018). Teacher talk in 40 secondary mathematics classrooms was analysed, comparing classes with low and high value-added scores in mathematics assessments. More evidence of metacognitive talk was found in the 20 high value-added classrooms and the specific features of metacognitive support through teacher talk which were more prevalent in these classrooms are summarised in Table 6b.

Table 6b Metacognitive teacher talk in high value-added classrooms (adapted from Zepeda et al, 2018)

Type of metacognitive support	Emphasis of teacher talk in high value-added mathematics classrooms
Metacognitive knowledge	Developing pupils' self-awareness of personal abilities and understanding (rather than how and when to apply strategies)
Metacognitive skills	Monitoring and evaluation phases of tasks (rather than the planning phase)
Metacognitive manner	Prompting through questions and directing (rather than modelling)
Metacognitive framing	Domain-general support, applicable in a variety of situations (rather than support related to specific problems or types of problem)

Although Zepeda et al acknowledge that cause and effect cannot be established here, as there may be other factors driving attainment and indeed the teacher talk itself, the study provides some insight into metacognitive aspects of talk that may be especially supportive. It is worth noting, however, the way that they are oriented to the context of mathematical problem-solving, a reminder of the arguments for such skills often being associated with subject content.

Drawing these three examples together, the implications are that effective metacognition both enhances pupil talk and arises from it, if appropriately structured. The use of metacognitive talk can be modelled by teachers in a subject-specific context and this may be associated with pupil attainment. One specific aspect of metacognition, according to Flavell (1979), is critical thinking and the final section of this chapter examines this in more depth.

6.5 How does classroom talk relate to developing pupils as critical thinkers?

The nature and importance of critical thinking

Willingham (2007) defines critical thinking as a form of reasoning, decision-making, and problem-solving which has three characteristics:

1. effectiveness: decision-making based in logical thought and avoiding common pitfalls;

2. novelty: the capacity to apply learning to a new situation;

3. self-direction: a process of thought led by the learner.

Willingham is also clear that the ability to go beyond the surface structure of an issue or problem depends on deep knowledge of subject matter and that the evidence for this being a skill transferable across domains is limited. Others have highlighted additional facets of critical thought. For example, Lipman (2003) stresses its practical, applied nature, Noddings (2006) takes a broad view of critical thought going beyond the academic, to encompass issues of personal belief with relevance to everyday life, while Fisher (2009) argues for the importance of attitudes, such as a willingness to challenge and a passion for truth.

In line with its inclusion in the OECD's (2018) global learning framework, Ritchhart (2015) reports on surveys of US employers, which suggests that applied skills, including critical thinking, are more highly rated than academic ones. In addition to basic employability, arguments have also been made that the ability to engage in critical debate may facilitate more general social mobility and active citizenship (Moorghen, 2016). As well as this Western perspective, the value of critical thinking has also been recognised more widely. In Singapore, known for its high performance in international comparisons, Tan (2017) discusses a national policy initiative at government level to embed critical thinking within curriculum areas. This is in response to concerns from employers about the impact of workers who are 'study-smart' but who lack criticality, showing the potential limitations of an educational focus solely on knowledge.

The role of talk in promoting critical thinking

Arguments for the role of talk in developing critical thinking come from a number of angles, but centre largely on talk's role in two processes: making thought visible and exposing different perspectives. Critical thinking is implicit in many of the models of talk from previous chapters, such as Collaborative Reasoning (Reznitskaya et al, 2009) and Reciprocal Teaching (Palinscar and Brown, 1984), which have in common structured engagement with ideas arising from a text and a gradual transition towards pupil regulation of the process. Murphy et al (2018) report on a similar talk-based programme, Quality Talk, specifically aimed at promoting critical analytic thinking. Like Collaborative Reasoning, Quality Talk is a small-group, teacher-facilitated discussion of a text based around a set of discourse moves intended to elicit this sort of thought. One of the distinctive features of this programme is its prescribed mini lessons. In a year-long intervention with elementary school pupils, the researchers found an improvement in pupils' use of critical talk and a suggestion of much stronger than average growth in individual comprehension. Also focusing on children's response to themes from literature and drawing on the concept of exploratory talk, Pierce and Gilles (2008) show how this has been used to develop 'critical conversations' in which pupils engage deeply with the text's issues. Their examination of classroom transcripts from learners aged between 6 and 13 yields four ways that critical talk may be nurtured to:

1. create a safe classroom community;

2. develop protocols for discussing difficult or sensitive issues;

3. embed critical discussion in curricular knowledge and materials;

4. identify and refer back to recurring discussion themes and events.

What is clear is the way that these points link to underlying principles of critical thinking, such as the importance of relevant subject knowledge and the need to acknowledge the affective dimension of such activities. It is also apparent that this research focuses on talk related to English as a discipline, rather than spanning a range of subjects or making claims for transferability. One well-researched form of talk to promote critical thought, which is potentially more generic in nature, is Philosophy for Children.

The example of Philosophy for Children

Philosophy for Children, commonly known as P4C, is an approach to learning originating in 1970 with Matthew Lipman. It centres on children learning through dialogue in a community of enquiry, thereby aiming for distributed thinking centred on critical thought and reasoning, but also creative and caring thinking (Lipman, 1998). Unlike similar forms of group dialogue, such as Collaborative Reasoning, P4C is distinguished by its focus on pupil-generated philosophical questions. The precise structure of a session was not prescribed by Lipman but has been enacted in a number of variations. Common features are: a starting activity, the sharing of a stimulus, pupils suggesting and deciding on enquiry questions, the enquiry dialogue itself and some form of review (Topping and Trickey, 2014). In its use of pupil-led, collective analysis of a novel dilemma, P4C, then, aligns closely with the hallmarks of critical thinking outlined earlier.

Due in part to its longevity, P4C has been extensively researched, in terms of impact both on talk itself and on other academic outcomes. The 'Thinking through Philosophy' form of P4C (eg Cleghorn, 2003) has been trialled in the UK and found to increase open questioning from the teacher, participation from the pupils and more elaborated, reasoned contributions from the pupils (Topping and Trickey, 2014), while the same research also yielded evidence of cognitive gains sustained two years after the intervention (Topping and Trickey, 2007). Reznitskaya et al (2012) report similar improvements in the quality of talk and pupil ownership in an experimental study in the US, but their research also questions transfer to pupils' subsequent individual reasoning. These authors speculate that more support in terms of longer exposure to P4C, experience of such dialogue in varied contexts and specific teacher guidance might help in this respect. In general, however, evidence for the impact of P4C on critical thought and reasoning is strong. Trickey and Topping's (2004) systematic review of 10 controlled outcome studies over a 30-year period in both primary and secondary schools found consistently positive effective sizes, mostly measured through reasoning tests. There is also a suggestion that benefits may go beyond reasoning itself into the wider curriculum, as the EEF's (2015) randomised control trial involving an intervention in 48 primary schools in England found a positive impact on attainment in reading and mathematics tests.

A class teacher implements classroom philosophy to develop critical thinking

Claire was a primary teacher who took part in piloting work for the 'Thinking through philosophy' materials discussed above. Her involvement was motivated by a desire to improve speaking and listening skills and particularly the use of dialogue as a learning tool. Claire began by introducing to her Years 5 and 6 class the concepts of philosophy and dialogue and by helping the children to categorise questions, identifying those which could not be answered conclusively, but could be explored. Other preparatory work included practising focusing exercises, proving or disproving statements and developing ground rules for building or challenging the views of others. In this way, the class gradually built up to full philosophy sessions. Once these were underway, skills cards were introduced each week, helping the children to reflect on and improve their critical thought by focusing their attention on processes such as changing their mind or asking questions for clarification. Over time, the children's articulated thinking became more sophisticated, as they justified their ideas and reasoned using language such as, 'That doesn't necessarily mean that...', or 'Have you got an example of what you mean by...?'. As their confidence increased, Claire was able to take a lower-key role, allowing pupils to debate increasingly independently. As well as the success of the philosophy lessons themselves, Claire noticed transferable outcomes elsewhere, as children realised that they had something to contribute in all lessons. Improved criticality, questioning, self-regulation and empathy were noticeable across the curriculum, as evidenced in English comprehension, mathematical reasoning and scientific enquiry.

6.6 Summary

Arguments have been made for twenty-first century learners to be equipped not only with knowledge, but also with attitudes and skills, including using technology, self-regulation and critical thinking. Questions have been raised over whether such skills are generic and transferable with a strong case for them being embedded in specific subject domains. Technology can be thought of as one means of generating dialogic space and promoting talk in distinctive ways, but this is best thought of as part of a wider view of dialogic learning. Much of the talk encountered in Chapters 3 to 5 has an inherently metacognitive dimension, bringing these processes to the surface, and metacognitive talk may also be associated with high-attaining classrooms. Many forms of talk promote critical thinking and P4C is a well-researched example with evidence of impact on reasoning but also wider attainment.

- In what ways do you, or might you, use technology to add value to your classroom by providing a stimulus or a space for new forms of dialogue?

- How might you explicitly model metacognitive processes through teacher-led talk?

- What does critical thought involve in a specific subject that you teach? To what extent is this different from other subjects?

Exploring further

SAPERE is a charity supporting P4C and its website offers guidance and resources across age phases:

- www.sapere.org.uk (accessed 17 May 2019).

Rupert Wegerif's book sums up much of the thinking and research linking dialogue and technology:

- Wegerif, R (2007) *Dialogic Teaching and Technology.* New York: Springer.

This site, created by an ICT curriculum development officer, includes examples of sites that can be used to create speech bubbles and characters as discussed in Section 6.3:

- https://blogs.glowscotland.org.uk/fa/ICTFalkirkPrimaries/comics-in-the-classroom-online-tools (accessed 17 May 2019).

Talkwall is a platform facilitating the sort of discussion between small groups introduced in Section 6.3:

- www.talkwall.net/#! (accessed 23 Aug 2019).

Chapter 7
Planning for action and implementation

7.1 Chapter overview

This chapter will outline:

7.2   the main findings about classroom talk;

7.3   working out what you want to achieve and how to turn priorities into actions;

7.4   implementing change and evaluating success.

7.2 What are the main findings about classroom talk?

Key messages for teachers from the evidence

Reviewing the evidence in this book, it is possible to discern a number of findings about classroom talk that seem to be well supported by evidence and worthy of your consideration. Some examples, in broad terms, include these insights.

- Although classroom interaction remains centred on teacher-dominated discourse that can be cognitively limiting, there are some clear ways of managing whole-class discussion more effectively. The third, 'feedback' move, in particular, can yield improvements in the quality of reasoning but also in attainment more widely (Chapter 3).

- Dialogic teaching can be developed initially by adopting this as an over-arching stance or ethos, as opposed to focusing on a single, all-encompassing form of talk. Nevertheless, some specific teacher interventions can improve the level of dialogic talk. If implemented over time, they can have an impact on attainment (Chapter 4).

- Pupils can be taught to engage in productive peer discussions through the use of explicit modelling and negotiated ground rules. Appropriate tasks and stimuli are critical, as is the active role played by the teacher. A number of structured programmes or models exist and benefits have been found for the quality of talk and for transfer to attainment in other areas (Chapter 5).

- Appropriately structured classroom talk can play an important role in the nurturing of other important aspects of learning such as metacognition and critical thinking. These skills can also be developed through the use of technology to create a 'dialogic space' (Chapter 6).

Limitations of the evidence

Before rushing to enact any of these principles, it is important to be aware of the limitations of the evidence. On the one hand, Mercer and Dawes (2014) argue that there is strong consensus about the types of talk that are most productive – in terms of participation and educational outcomes – and the sorts of strategies likely to foster this. Nevertheless, Howe and Abedin's (2013) systematic review suggests that the research field has not necessarily progressed in recent years in ways that might have the most impact. Given the resilience of fairly limited forms of interaction, particularly as reflected in Chapter 3, there is a sense that the argument for using talk more ambitiously and productively has not yet been made with sufficient force. As Resnick and Schantz (2015) point out, embedded 'recitation' practices are based on strongly held assumptions, such as the view that only some forms of instruction and some learners can be associated with high-level reasoning and intelligence that can be grown. The case for transferable academic benefits is therefore a crucial one to make if dialogic teaching is to be a 'game changer' (p 443).

There are two main, inter-related limitations to the current body of research, as explored by Howe and Abedin (2013). One concerns the distinction between model-based and target-based evaluations. A large number of studies focus on assessing talk in terms of fidelity to a pre-determined model and, as noted by Murphy et al (2009), these models are sometimes the researcher's own. An issue here is that, even if positive outcomes are found, this sort of research cannot determine the extent to which one model has more potential than another. Target-based assessment, involving external criteria such as academic attainment, could allow this sort of comparison but there are relatively few studies focusing on the outcomes of dialogue in this way, particularly in the area of whole-class interaction. While some exist, the case for more studies establishing and replicating causal connections between spoken language and learning has been specifically made (Reznitskaya and Gregory, 2013; Resnick and Schantz, 2015). This links to the other key issue, which is one of scale and methodology. The nature of spoken language lends itself to in-depth, qualitative analysis, which tends to be on a small scale. While there are questions over the appropriateness of quantitative methods for the meaningful study of classroom talk, there are strong arguments for their use in larger studies which would allow the magnitude of impact to be gauged more clearly (Howe and Abedin, 2013). As emphasised by Mercer and Dawes (2014), this is not to suggest the inherent superiority of studies of this kind, but the need for this as part of a well-rounded body of research.

7.3 What do you want to achieve?

Choosing priorities

This book has covered many aspects of classroom talk, so it is important to be clear about your priorities. For example, do you want to:

- promote pupils' proficiency in spoken communication?
- increase pupils' confidence in sharing ideas?
- develop collaboration as a social skill?
- develop collaboration as a means to problem-solving?
- improve pupils' individual reasoning skills?
- encourage pupils to enquire and explore issues with others?
- generate a deep understanding of concepts taught?
- find out more about pupils' own thinking and ideas by allowing space for this?
- enhance pupils' metacognitive skills?
- create more equitable classrooms in which power is more evenly distributed?

Prioritising these diverse, but inter-related, outcomes is an important first step and a list such as this may be a useful tool for an initial whole-staff discussion. The remainder of this chapter considers ways of putting a small number of priorities into practice.

Planning for action

Given the arguments reflected in Chapter 1 about generic limitations of educational research and the more specific points mentioned in this chapter about the evidence around talk, it is important for you to be clear about what is the most productive way forward. Reflecting on these uncertainties, Wiliam (2017) identifies four roles that education research can claim, providing a useful starting point for action. Educational research can, he argues:

1. suggest what is likely to be ineffective and unworthy of attention;
2. help to weigh up potential benefits against financial costs;

3. draw attention to the specific conditions in which a strategy may work;

4. focus attention and professional development on changes likely to have a positive impact.

Wiliam's (2017) principles can be related to the oracy case study from Woodside Academy presented in Section 2.5. Table 7a shows how this might be translated into school-level action.

Table 7a Key actions in planning for change

Key action	Why is this important?
Take stock of the current use of spoken language in the classroom	There may be many strong features of current practice that should be acknowledged and it is also important to be clear about the specific aims relating to spoken language. For Woodside, this centred on raising aspirations and life opportunities.
Share key findings on promising strategies from research with colleagues	As well as a starting point at school level, it is important to draw on existing evidence in terms of what is worthy of attention. At Woodside, this was mediated through resources and training from an external provider.
Decide on a small number of advocates for change	Personal testimony from colleagues is powerful and it is important that this is not associated with a single school leader. Woodside launched their work with a first tier of teachers to generate and trial new practices.
Select a manageable approach and appropriate resources	Thoughtful integration of new practices into everyday work helps to minimise new workload and takes into account the specific conditions of each school. At Woodside, oracy criteria for each year group were created, for example, along with a new planning format.
Invite colleagues to see and hear about new practices	Creating an atmosphere of trust in which colleagues can observe one another's classrooms allows for the sharing of new practices. Lead teachers at Woodside invited others to experience first-hand their modelled lessons, rich in spoken language.

| Consider practices which may be feasible and cost-effective to implement more widely | A whole-school approach allows for coherent implementation of strategies likely to work in these conditions, but it is important also to retain a level of professional judgment for individual teachers. Oracy assumed a high status at Woodside through assemblies and performance management, but classes negotiated their own talk charters and selected strategies fit for purpose. |

7.4 How will you know when you have achieved it?

As well as implementing new practices, you may be ready for a more systematic approach to intervention, involving an evaluation of success. As seen throughout this book, successful classroom talk can be defined in a number of ways. For example, studies cited have variously focused on outcomes including:

- authentic pupil participation (eg Burns and Myhill, 2004);

- the amount of productive talk generated (eg Michaels et al, 2008);

- the benefits for thinking or reasoning (eg Reznitskaya et al, 2009);

- the transferable impact on wider attainment (eg Alexander, 2018).

One approach to evaluation is to follow a cyclical model such as that used in action research.

An action research perspective

Action research, often traced back to Lewin's (1946) work on social change, has been defined as: '*The study of a social situation with a view to improving the quality of action within it*' (Elliott, 1991, p 69). Action research has been interpreted and implemented in many ways and is extensively documented elsewhere (eg Townsend, 2013). The common feature across the various models proposed is a series of cycles involving the following in some form:

Figure 7a The action research cycle

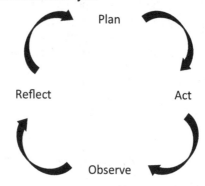

Action research is predominantly associated with small-scale, often context-specific, insider enquiry addressing an issue through a recursive process of developing a focus, reconnaissance, planned intervention, evidence gathering and reflection, ideally conducted collaboratively (Townsend, 2013). Much of this process is evident in the following case study.

Case study

A whole-school enquiry approach

At Tower Street Primary School, the leadership team have taken the decision to move from evaluating teaching and learning through graded lesson observations to a more empowering, enquiry-based approach, focused on gathering evidence of progress over time.

Table 7b An enquiry process at Tower Street

Tower Street's activities	Action research phase
Every year, teacher research groups are set up, each comprising teachers, teaching assistants and a senior leader as a 'knowledgeable other'. The research focus for the year is determined partly by school data and is initiated by a research text accessible to all. One recent focus, launched through Robin Alexander's work (eg Alexander, 2017), has been promoting more dialogic practice in classrooms.	Identifying a focus and conducting reconnaissance

A clear structure for the year is established, including designated staff meeting time for launching, monitoring and evaluating the interventions and cover for planned-for peer observations. Enquiry questions have centred on issues such as structured group talk, the use of dialogue to improve comprehension skills and increasing 'wait time' after questions.	Planning for action
Impact is assessed chiefly through data from peer observations and questionnaires. As well as the school's teaching staff, the process has involved governors, colleagues from a local innovation hub and a contact at a nearby university.	Implementing and observing actions
Termly action plans are produced and dissemination takes place through a midpoint review and a poster presentation of findings, before another cycle of work begins. Developing a critical response from teachers to enquiry findings remains a challenge, but the increase in ownership and collaboration is helping to foster a culture within the school of evidence-informed professional development and school improvement.	Reflecting on and evaluating change

The action-research perspective, even if not followed to its fullest extent, offers a number of insights. Firstly, the emphasis on identifying an issue and conducting reconnaissance suggests that a productive starting point for action is to *identify a problem or issue to be addressed*. For example, in Chapter 1, arguments for talk were presented in not only academic terms but also social and political ones and each of these relates to a particular part of the evidence-base. Having settled on a purpose for talk, carried out some reconnaissance and decided on an evidence-informed strategy, action research emphasises the evaluation of evidence as *a reflective and collaborative endeavour*, geared towards a deep understanding of a specific setting. This is in contrast to a view of success measured solely by a snapshot of attainment, for example. Finally, this perspective centres on *a cyclical, iterative process*. Many of the possibilities for improved talk outlined in this book, such as the development of exploratory talk (Mercer and Littleton, 2007) or the nurturing of a dialogic classroom ethos (Alexander, 2017) are outcomes requiring sustained engagement, refined over a period of time.

7.5 Summary

There are a number of potentially fruitful aspects of classroom talk, well supported by evidence, for teachers to explore. These include developing the feedback, or evaluation, move in whole-class questioning and the teaching of skills for productive peer dialogue. Nevertheless, it is important to note the limitations of what is known. Specifically, there is a need for larger-scale studies and a target-based focus on transferable outcomes beyond congruence with a particular model of talk. Bearing in mind the often situated nature of knowledge about education, action should not involve the implementation of universal principles, but a careful consideration of specific contexts. One approach to evaluating the success of any actions is therefore to conceive of an intervention as a process of reflective enquiry.

Questions for enquiry in your own school

- What examples of good practice in classroom talk exist already in your context?

- Building on this, what talk-related goals are most appropriate and why?

- What sort of initial change would be feasible to implement as a first step?

- What outcomes would constitute success?

Exploring further

The Education Endowment Foundation has produced an implementation guide to help schools turn evidence into school-wide action:

- https://educationendowmentfoundation.org.uk/tools/guidance-reports/a-schools-guide-to-implementation (accessed 17 May 2019).

This paper by Paul Thompson reports specifically on practitioner enquiry as a means of developing classroom talk, identifying factors that may help or hinder this process:

- Thompson, P (2007) Developing Classroom Talk Through Practitioner Research. *Educational Action Research*, 15(1): 41–60.

References

Adey, P and Shayer, M (2015) The Effects of Cognitive Acceleration. In Resnick, L, Asterhan, C and Clarke, S (eds) *Socializing Intelligence Through Academic Talk and Dialogue* (pp 127–40). Washington, DC: AERA.

Adey, P, Shayer, M and Yates, C (2003) *Thinking Science: Professional Edition.* London: Nelson Thornes.

Aguiar, O, Mortimer, E and Scott, P (2010) Learning From and Responding to Students' Questions: The Authoritative and Dialogic Tension. *Journal of Research in Science Teaching,* 47(2): 174–93.

Alexander, R (2000) *Culture and Pedagogy: International Comparisons in Primary Education.* Oxford: Blackwell.

Alexander, R (2003) Talk in Teaching and Learning: International Perspectives, in Qualifications and Curriculum Authority (ed) *New Perspectives on English in the Classroom* (pp 27–37). London: QCA.

Alexander, R (2004) *Talk for Learning: the Second Year.* North Allerton: North Yorkshire County Council. [online] Available at: www.robinalexander.org.uk/wp-content/uploads/2017/10/North-Yorks-report-04.pdf (accessed 30 June 2019).

Alexander, R (2008) Culture, Dialogue and Learning: Notes on an Emerging Pedagogy. In Mercer, N and Hodkinson, S (eds) *Exploring Talk in School* (pp 91–114). London: Sage.

Alexander, R (ed) (2010) *Children, Their World, Their Education: Final Report and Recommendations of the Cambridge Primary Review.* Abingdon: Routledge.

Alexander, R (2012) *Improving Oracy and Classroom Talk in English Schools: Achievements and Challenges: Extended and Referenced Version of a Presentation Given at the DfE Seminar on Oracy, the National Curriculum and Educational Standards, 20 February 2012.* [online] Available at: www.robinalexander.org.uk/wp-content/uploads/2012/06/DfE-oracy-120220-Alexander-FINAL.pdf (accessed 30 June 2019).

Alexander, R (2014) Evidence, Policy and the Reform of Primary Education: a Cautionary Tale. *Forum,* 56(3): 349–76.

Alexander, R (2017) *Towards Dialogic Teaching: Rethinking Classroom Talk.* 5th edition. York: Dialogos.

Alexander, R (2018) Developing Dialogic Teaching: Genesis, Process, Trial. *Research Papers in Education,* 33(5): 561–98.

Applebee, A, Langer, J, Nystrand, M and Gamoran, A (2003) Discussion-based Approaches to Developing Understanding: Classroom Instruction and Student Performance in Middle and High School English. *American Educational Research Journal,* 40(3): 685–730.

Asterhan, C (2015) Introducing Online Dialogues in Co-located Classrooms: If, Why and How. In Resnick, L, Asterhan, C and Clarke, S (eds) *Socializing Intelligence Through Academic Talk and Dialogue* (pp 205–18). Washington, DC: AERA.

Atherton, C (2018) *Assessment: Evidence-based Teaching for Enquiring Teachers.* St Albans: Critical Publishing.

Baines, E, Blatchford, P and Kutnick, P (2008) Pupil Grouping for Learning: Developing a Social Pedagogy of the Classroom. In Gillies, R, Ashman, A, Terwel, J (eds) *The Teacher's Role in Developing Cooperative Learning in the Classroom.* New York: Springer.

Baines, E, Blatchford, P and Webster, P (2015) The Challenges of Implementing Group Work in Primary School Classrooms and Including Pupils With Special Educational Needs. *Education, 3–13,* 43(1): 15–29.

Baines, E, Rubie-Davies, C and Blatchford, P (2009) Improving Pupil Group Work Interaction and Dialogue in Primary Classrooms: Results From a Year-Long Intervention Study. *Cambridge Journal of Education,* 39(1): 95–117.

Bakhtin, M (1981) *The Dialogic Imagination: Four Essays.* Austin: University of Texas Press.

Bakhtin, M (1986) *Speech Genres and Other Late Essays.* Austin: University of Texas Press.

Barnes, D (1976) *From Communication to Curriculum.* London: Penguin.

Barnes, D (2008) Exploratory Talk for Learning. In Mercer, N and Hodkinson, S (eds) *Exploring Talk in School* (pp 1–15). London: Sage.

Barnes, D and Todd, F (1977) *Communication and Learning in Small Groups.* London: Routledge.

Barnett, S and Ceci, S (2002) When and Where Do We Apply What We Learn? A Taxonomy for Far Transfer. *Psychological Bulletin,* 128: 612–37.

Bercow, J (2008) *The Bercow Report: A Review of Services for Children and Young People (0–19) with Speech, Language and Communication Needs.* London: Department for Children Schools and Families (DCSF). [online]

Available at: https://dera.ioe.ac.uk/8405/7/7771-dcsf-bercow_Redacted.pdf (accessed 30 June 2019).

Bernstein, B (1971) *Class, Codes and Control*. St Albans: Paladin.

Biesta, G (2016) Improving Education Through Research? From Effectiveness, Causality and Technology to Purpose, Complexity and Culture. *Policy Futures in Education*, 14(2): 194–210.

Bisra, K, Liu, Q, Nesbit, J, Salimi, F and Winne, P (2018) Inducing Self-explanation: A Meta-Analysis. *Educational Psychology Review*, 30: 703–25.

Black, P and Wiliam, D (1998a) Assessment and Classroom Learning. *Assessment in Education: Principles, Policy and Practice*, 5(1): 7–74.

Black, P and Wiliam, D (1998b) Inside the Black Box: Raising Standards Through Classroom Assessment. *Phi Delta Kappa*, October 1998: 1–13.

Black, P and Wiliam, D (2018) Classroom Assessment and Pedagogy. *Assessment in Education: Principles, Policy and Practice*, 25(6): 551–75.

Blatchford, P, Kutnick, P, Baines, E and Galton, M (2003) Towards a Social Pedagogy of Classroom Group Work. *International Journal of Educational Research*, 39: 153–72.

Boyd, M and Markarian, W (2011) Dialogic Teaching: Talk in Service of a Dialogic Stance. *Language and Education*, 25(6): 515–34.

British Educational Research Association (BERA) (2014) *Research and the Teaching Profession: Building the Capacity for a Self-improving Education System*. [online] Available at: www.bera.ac.uk/wp-content/uploads/2013/12/BERA-RSA-Research-Teaching-Profession-FULL-REPORT-for-web.pdf?noredirect=1 (accessed 30 June 2019).

Bruner, J (1978) The Role of Dialogue in Language Acquisition. In Sinclair, A, Jevella, R and Levelt, W (eds) *The Child's Conception of Language* (pp 241–56). Berlin: Springer-Verlag.

Bullock, A (1975) *The Bullock Report: a Language for Life: Report of the Committee of Enquiry Appointed by the Secretary of State for Education and Science Under the Chairmanship of Sir Alan Bullock FBA*. London: HMSO.

Burns, C and Myhill, D (2004) Interactive or Inactive? A Consideration of the Nature of Interaction in Whole Class Teaching. *Cambridge Journal of Education*, 34(1): 35–49.

Cain, T (2015) Teachers' Engagement With Published Research: Addressing the Knowledge Problem. *The Curriculum Journal*, 26(3): 488–509.

Calcagni, E and Lago, L (2018) The Three Domains for Dialogue: A Framework for Analysing Dialogic Approaches to Teaching and Learning. *Learning, Culture and Social Interaction*, 18: 1–12.

Cameron, D (2003) Schooling Spoken Language: Beyond 'Communication'. In Qualifications and Curriculum Authority (ed) *New Perspectives on English in the Classroom* (pp 64–72). London: QCA.

Carter, R (2003) The Grammar of Talk: Spoken English, Grammar and the Classroom. In Qualifications and Curriculum Authority (ed) *New Perspectives on English in the Classroom* (pp 5–13). London: QCA.

Carter, R (2004) *Language and Creativity: The Art of Common Talk*. London: Routledge.

Cazden, C (2001) *Classroom Discourse: The Language of Teaching and Learning*. 2nd edition. Portsmouth, NH: Heinemann.

Centre for Social Justice (2014) *Closing the Divide: Tackling Educational Inequality in England*. [online] Available at: www.centreforsocialjustice.org.uk/library/closing-divide-tackling-educational-inequality-england (accessed 30 June 2019).

Chambers, F and Armour, K (2011) Do As We Do and Not As We Say: Teacher Educators Supporting Student Teachers to Learn on Teaching Practice. *Sport, Education and Society*, 16(4): 527–44.

Clark, A, Anderson, R, Kuo, L, Kim, I, Archodidou, A and Nguyen-Jahiel, K (2003) Collaborative Reasoning: Expanding Ways For Children to Talk and Think in School. *Educational Psychology Review*, 15(2): 181–98.

Claxton, G (2008) *What's the Point of School? Rediscovering the Heart of Education*. Richmond: Oneworld.

Cleghorn, P (2003) *Thinking Through Philosophy 3: A Programme In Thinking Skills and Emotional Intelligence*. Blackburn: Educational Printing Services Limited.

Collins, A and White, B (2015) How Technology is Broadening the Nature of Learning Dialogues. In Resnick, L, Asterhan, C and Clarke, S (eds) *Socializing Intelligence Through Academic Talk and Dialogue* (pp 231–9). Washington, DC: AERA.

Communication Trust (2013) *A Generation Adrift*. London: The Communication Trust.

Connolly, P, Keenan, C and Urbanska, K (2018) The Trials of Evidence-based Practice in Education: A Systematic Review of Randomised Control Trials in Education Research 1980–2016. *Educational Research*, 60(3): 276–91.

Cook, V, Warwick, P, Vrikki, M, Major, L and Wegerif, R (2019) Developing Material-dialogic Space in Geography Learning and Teaching: Combining a Dialogic Pedagogy With the Use of a Microblogging Tool. *Thinking Skills and Creativity*, 31: 217–31.

Coultas, V (2012) Classroom Talk: Are We Listening to Teachers' Voices? *English in Education*, 46(2): 175–89.

Coultas, V (2015) Revisiting Debates on Oracy: Classroom Talk – Moving Towards a Democratic Pedagogy? *Changing English*, 22(1): 72–86.

Dawes, L, Mercer, N and Wegerif, R (2004) *Thinking Together: A Programme of Activities for Developing Speaking, Listening and Thinking Skills for Children Aged 8–11*. Birmingham: Imaginative Minds.

DfE (2010) *The Importance of Teaching: The Schools White Paper 2010*. London: TSO.

DfE (2013) National Curriculum in England: English Programmes of Study. [online] Available at: www.gov.uk/government/publications/national-curriculum-in-england-english-programmes-of-study (accessed 30 June 2019).

DfE (2016) Eliminating Unnecessary Workload Around Marking: Report of the Independent Teacher Workload Review Group. [online] Available at: https://assets.publishing.service.gov.uk/government/uploads/system/uploads/attachment_data/file/511256/Eliminating-unnecessary-workload-around-marking.pdf (accessed 30 June 2019).

Early Intervention Foundation (2017) *Language As a Child Wellbeing Indicator*. [online] Available at: www.eif.org.uk/report/language-as-a-child-wellbeing-indicator (accessed 30 June 2019).

Education Endowment Foundation (EEF) (2015) *Philosophy for Children: Evaluation Report and Executive Summary*. London: Education Endowment Foundation.

Education Endowment Foundation (EEF) (2017) *Dialogic Teaching: Evaluation Report and Executive Summary*. London: Education Endowment Foundation.

Education Endowment Foundation (EEF) (2018a) Metacognition and Self-Regulation: Teaching and Learning Toolkit. [online] Available at: https://educationendowmentfoundation.org.uk/pdf/generate/?u=https://educationendowmentfoundation.org.uk/pdf/toolkit/?id=138&t=Teaching%20and%20Learning%20Toolkit&e=138&s= (accessed 30 June 2019).

Education Endowment Foundation (EEF) (2018b) *Metacognition and Self-regulated Learning: Guidance Report*. London: Education Endowment Foundation.

Edwards, A and Furlong, V (1978) *The Language of Teaching*. London: Heinemann.

Edwards, A and Westgate, D (1994) *Investigating Classroom Talk*. 2nd edition. London: Routledge Falmer.

Edwards, J (2009) Socio-Constructivist and Socio-Cultural Lenses on Collaborative Peer Talk in a Secondary Mathematics Classroom, *Proceedings of the British Society for Research into Learning Mathematics*, 29(1): 49–54.

Elliott, J (1991) *Action Research for Educational Change*. Milton Keynes: Open University Press.

Elliott, V, Baird, J, Hopfenbeck, T, Ingram, J, Thompson, I, Usher, N, Zantout, M, Richardson, J and Coleman, R (2016) *A Marked Improvement? A Review of the Evidence on Written Marking*. London: Education Endowment Foundation. [online] Available at: https://educationendowmentfoundation.org.uk/public/files/Presentations/Publications/EEF_Marking_Review_April_2016.pdf (accessed 18 July 2019).

English Speaking Union (2017) *International Perspectives on Oracy*. [online] Available at: www.esu.org/blog/international-perspectives-on-oracy (accessed 30 June 2019).

Fernández, M, Wegerif, R, Mercer, N and Rojas-Drummond, S (2015) Re-conceptualizing 'Scaffolding' and the Zone of Proximal Development in the Context of Symmetrical Collaborative Learning. *The Journal of Classroom Interaction*, 50(1): 54–72.

Fisher, R (2009) *Creative Dialogue: Talk for Thinking in the Classroom*. Abingdon: Routledge.

Fisher, R and Larkin, S (2008) Pedagogy or Ideological Struggle? An Examination of Pupils' and Teachers' Expectations for Talk in the Classroom. *Language and Education*, 22(1): 1–16.

Flanders, N (1961) Analysing Teacher Behaviour. *Educational Leadership*, December 1961: 173–200.

Flavell, J (1979) Metacognition and Cognitive Monitoring: A New Area of Cognitive-Developmental Inquiry. *American Psychologist*, 34(10): 906–11.

Freire, P (1970) *Pedagogy of the Oppressed*. London: Penguin.

Galton, M, Hargreaves, L, Comber, C, Wall, D and Pell, T (1999) Changes in Patterns of Teacher Interaction in Primary Classrooms 1976–96. *British Educational Research Journal*, 25(1): 23–37.

Galton, M, Simon, B and Croll, P (1980) *Inside the Primary Classroom*. London: Routledge.

Gaunt, A and Stott, A (2019) *Transform Teaching and Learning Through Talk: The Oracy Imperative*. London: Rowman & Littlefield.

Gilkerson, J, Richards, J, Warren, S, Kimbrough Oller, D, Russo, R and Vohr, B (2018) Language Experience in the Second Year of Life and Language Outcomes in Late Childhood. *Pediatrics*, 142(4): 1–11.

Gillies, R (2016) *Enhancing Classroom-based Talk: Blending Practice, Research and Theory*. Abingdon: Routledge.

Gillies, R and Boyle, M (2008) Teachers' Discourse During Co-operative Learning and Their Perceptions of This Pedagogical Practice. *Teaching and Teacher Education*, 24: 1333–48.

Goswami, U (2015) *Children's Cognitive Development and Learning: Cambridge Primary Review Trust Research Survey 3*. Cambridge: University of Cambridge.

Greeno, J (2015) Classroom Talk Sequences and Learning. In Resnick, L, Asterhan, C and Clarke, S (eds) *Socializing Intelligence Through Academic Talk and Dialogue* (pp 255–62). Washington, DC: AERA.

Hardman, F (2008) Teachers' Use of Feedback in Whole-Class and Group-based Talk. In Mercer, N and Hodkinson, S (eds) *Exploring Talk in School* (pp 131–50). London: Sage.

Hattie, J (2009) *Visible Learning: A Synthesis of Over 800 Meta-Analyses Relating to Achievement*. Abingdon: Routledge.

Hattie, J (2012) *Visible Learning for Teachers: Maximising Impact on Learning*. Abingdon: Routledge.

Hattie, J and Timperley, H (2007) The Power of Feedback. *Review of Educational Research*, 77(1): 81–112.

Hattie, J and Yates, G (2014) *Visible Learning and the Science of How We Learn*. Abingdon: Routledge.

Heath, S B (1983) *Ways With Words: Language, Life and Work in Communities and Classrooms*. Cambridge: Cambridge University Press.

Hennessy, S (2011) The Role of Digital Artefacts on the Interactive Whiteboard in Supporting Classroom Dialogue. *Journal of Computer Assisted Learning*, 27: 463–89.

Higham, R, Brindley, S and Van de Pol, J (2014) Shifting the Primary Focus: Assessing the Case for Dialogic Education in Secondary Classrooms. *Language and Education*, 28(1): 86–99.

Hirsch, E (2009) *The Making of Americans: Democracy and our Schools*. New Haven: Yale University Press.

Hmelo-Silver, C, Duncan, R and Chinn, C (2007) Scaffolding and Achievement in Problem-based and Inquiry Learning: A Response to Kirschner, Sweller and Clark (2006). *Educational Psychologist*, 42(2): 99–107.

Howe, C (2014) Optimizing Small Group Discourse in Classrooms: Effective Practices and Theoretical Constraints. *International Journal of Education Research*, 63: 107–15.

Howe, C and Abedin, M (2013) Classroom Dialogue: A Systematic Review Across Four Decades of Research. *Cambridge Journal of Education*, 43(3): 325–56.

Howe, C, Hennessy, S, Mercer, N, Vrikki, M and Wheatley, L (2019) Teacher–Student Dialogue During Classroom Teaching: Does It Really Impact on Student Outcomes? *Journal of the Learning Sciences*, doi.org/10.17863/CAM.37142.

International Baccalaureate Organization (IBO) (2013) *What is an IB Education?* Cardiff: International Baccalaureate Organisation. [online] Available at: www.ibo.org/globalassets/what-is-an-ib-education-2017-en.pdf (accessed 18 July 2019).

Ingram, J and Elliott, V (2016) A Critical Analysis of the Role of Wait Time in Classroom Interactions and the Effects on Student and Teacher Interactional Behaviours. *Cambridge Journal of Education*, 46(1): 37–53.

Iordanou, K (2013) Developing Face-to-Face Argumentation Skills: Does Arguing on the Computer Help? *Journal of Cognition and Development*, 14(2): 292–320.

Kawalkar, A and Vijapurkar, J (2013) Scaffolding Science Talk: The Role of Teachers' Questions in the Inquiry Classroom. *International Journal of Science Education*, 35(12): 2004–27.

Keefer, M, Zeitz, C and Resnick, L (2000) Judging the Quality of Peer-led Student Dialogues. *Cognition and Instruction*, 18(1): 53–81.

Kershner, R, Mercer, N, Warwick, P and Kleine Staarman, J (2010) Can the Interactive Whiteboard Support Young Children's Collaborative Communication and Thinking in Classroom Science Activities? *Computer-Supported Collaborative Learning*, 5: 359–83.

Khong, T, Saito, E and Gillies, R (2017) Key Issues in Productive Classroom Talk and Interventions. *Educational Review*, 71(3): 334–49.

Kim, M and Wilkinson, I (2019) What is Dialogic Teaching? Constructing, Deconstructing, and Reconstructing a Pedagogy of Classroom Talk. *Learning Culture and Social Interaction*, 21: 70–86.

Kirschner, P, Sweller, J and Clark, R (2006) Why Minimal Guidance During Instruction Does Not Work: An Analysis of the Failure of Constructivist, Discovery, Problem-based, Experiential and Inquiry-based Learning. *Educational Psychologist*, 41(2): 75–86.

Kirschner, P, Sweller, J, Kirschner, F and Zambrano, J (2018) From Cognitive Load Theory to Collaborative Cognitive Load Theory. *International Journal of Computer Supported Collaborative Learning*, 13: 213–33.

Kleine Staarman, J (2009) The Joint Negotiation of Ground Rules: Establishing a Shared Collaborative Practice With New Educational Technology. *Language and Education*, 23(1): 79–95.

Kuhn, D and Zillmer, N (2015) Developing Norms of Discourse. In Resnick, L, Asterhan, C and Clarke, S (eds) *Socializing Intelligence Through Academic Talk And Dialogue* (pp 77–86). Washington, DC: AERA.

Lai, E (2011) *Metacognition: A Literature Review*. Pearson Assessments Research Reports. [online] Available at: https://images.pearsonassessments.com/images/tmrs/Metacognition_Literature_Review_Final.pdf (accessed 30 June 2019).

Lave, J and Wenger, E (1991) *Situated Learning: Legitimate Peripheral Participation*. Cambridge: Cambridge University Press.

Lefstein, A and Snell, J (2014) *Better Than Best Practice: Developing Teaching and Learning Through Dialogue*. Abingdon: Routledge.

Lemke, J (1990) *Talking Science*. Norwood, NJ: Ablex.

Lewin, K (1946) Action Research and Minority Problems. *Journal of Social Issues*, 2(4): 34–46.

Lipman, M (1998) Teaching Students to Think Reasonably: Some Findings of the Philosophy for Children Program. *The Clearing House: A Journal of Educational Strategies, Issues and Ideas*, 71(5): 277–80.

Lipman, M (2003) *Thinking in Education*. 2nd edition. Cambridge: Cambridge University Press.

Littleton, K and Mercer, N (2013) *Interthinking: Putting Talk to Work*. Abingdon: Routledge.

Loughran, J (2010) *What Expert Teachers Do: Enhancing Professional Knowledge for Classroom Practice*. Abingdon: Routledge.

Major, L, Warwick, P, Rasmussen, I, Ludvigsen, S and Cook, V (2018) Classroom Dialogue and Digital Technologies: A Scoping Review. *Educational Information Technology*, 23: 1995–2028.

Maybin, J (2006) *Children's Voices*. Basingstoke: Palgrave Macmillan.

McKenna, J (2017) *Your Child May Need This Skill As Much As Numeracy Or Literacy*. [online] Available at: www.weforum.org/agenda/2017/09/oracy-literacy-skill-every-child-needs (accessed 30 June 2019).

McKeown, M and Beck, I (2015) Effective Classroom Talk *is* Reading Comprehension Instruction. In Resnick, L, Asterhan, C and Clarke, S (eds) *Socializing Intelligence Through Academic Talk and Dialogue* (pp 51–62). Washington, DC: AERA.

Mehan, H (1979) What Time is it Denise? Asking Known Information Questions in Classroom Discourse. *Theory Into Practice*, 18(4): 285–94.

Mehan, H and Cazden, C (2015) The Study of Classroom Discourse: Early History and Current Developments. In Resnick, L, Asterhan, C and Clarke, S (eds) *Socializing Intelligence Through Academic Talk and Dialogue* (pp 13–34). Washington, DC: AERA.

Mercer, N (1995) *The Guided Construction of Knowledge: Talk Amongst Teachers and Learners*. Clevedon: Multilingual Matters.

Mercer, N (2000) *Words and Minds: How We Use Language to Think Together*. London: Routledge.

Mercer, N (2010) The Analysis of Classroom Talk: Methods and Methodologies. *British Journal of Educational Psychology*, 80: 1–14.

Mercer, N (2015) Why Oracy Must Be in the Curriculum (and Group Work in the Classroom). *Forum*, 57(1): 67–74.

Mercer, N (2018) *Oracy Education and Dialogic Teaching: What's the Difference?* [online] Available at: https://oracycambridge.org/2018/02/22/oracy-education-and-dialogic-teaching-whats-the-difference (accessed 30 June 2019).

Mercer, N and Dawes, L (2008) The Value of Exploratory Talk. In Mercer, N and Hodkinson, S (eds) *Exploring Talk in School* (pp 55–72). London: Sage.

Mercer, N and Dawes, L (2014) The Study of Talk Between Teachers and Students From the 1970s until the 2010s. *Oxford Review of Education*, 40(4): 430–45.

Mercer, N, Dawes, L and Kleine Staarman, J (2009) Dialogic Teaching in the Primary Science Classroom. *Language and Education*, 23 (4): 353–69.

Mercer, N, Hennessy, S and Warwick, P (2017a) Dialogue: Thinking Together and Digital Technology in the Classroom: Some Educational Implications of a Continuing Line of Inquiry. *International Journal of Educational Research*. [online] Available at: https://doi.org/10.1016/j.ijer.2017.08.007 (accessed 29 August 2019).

Mercer, N and Littleton, K (2007) *Dialogue and the Development of Children's Thinking: A Sociocultural Approach*. Abingdon: Routledge.

Mercer, N, Warwick, P and Ahmed, A (2017b) An Oracy Assessment Toolkit: Linking Research and Development in the Assessment of Students' Spoken Language Skills at Age 11–12. *Learning and Instruction*, 48: 51–60.

Michaels, S and O'Connor, C (2015) Conceptualizing Talk Moves As Tools: Professional Development Approaches for Academically Productive Discussions. In Resnick, L, Asterhan, C and Clarke, S (eds) *Socializing Intelligence Through Academic Talk and Dialogue* (pp 347–61). Washington, DC: AERA.

Michaels, S, O'Connor, C and Resnick, L (2008) Deliberative Discourse Idealized and Realized: Accountable Talk in the Classroom and in Civic Life. *Studies in the Philosophy of Education*, 27: 283–97.

Millard, W and Menzies, L (2016) *Oracy: The State of Speaking in our Schools*. London: Voice 21. [online] Available at: www.lkmco.org/wp-content/uploads/2016/11/Oracy-Report-Final.pdf (accessed 18 July).

Molinari, L, Maeli, C and Gnisi, A (2013) A Sequential Analysis of Classroom Discourse in Italian Primary Schools: The Many Faces of the IRF Pattern. *British Journal of Educational Psychology*, 83: 414–30.

Moorghen, A (2016) Oracy Through Debate, in Voice 21 and English Speaking Union. *Speaking Frankly: The Case for Oracy in the Curriculum*: 62–7.

Mortimer, E and Scott, P (2003) *Meaning Making in Secondary Science Classrooms*. Maidenhead: Open University Press.

Mroz, M, Smith, F and Hardman, F (2000) The Discourse of the Literacy Hour. *Cambridge Journal of Education*, 30(3): 379–90.

Mugny, G and Doise, W (1978) Socio-Cognitive Conflict and Structure of Individual and Collective Performances. *European Journal of Social Psychology*, 8: 181–92.

Murphy, P, Greene, J, Firetto, C, Hendrick, B, Li, M, Montalbano, C and Wei, L (2018) Quality Talk: Developing Students' Discourse to Promote High-Level Comprehension. *American Educational Research Journal*, 55(5): 1113–60.

Murphy, P, Wilkinson, I, Soter, A and Hennessey, M (2009) Examining the Effects of Classroom Discussion on Students' Comprehension of Text: A Meta-Analysis. *Journal of Educational Psychology*, 101(3): 740–64.

Myhill, D (2006) Talk, Talk, Talk: Teaching and Learning in Whole Class Discourse. *Research Papers in Education*, 21(1): 19–41.

Myhill, D and Warren, P (2005) Scaffolds or Straitjackets? Critical Moments in Classroom Discourse. *Educational Review*, 57(1): 55–69.

Naylor, S and Keogh, B (2013) Concept Cartoons: What Have We Learnt? *Journal of Turkish Science Education*, 10(1): 3–11.

Newman, R (2017) Engaging Talk: One Teacher's Scaffolding of Collaborative Talk. *Language and Education*, 31(2): 130–51.

Noddings, N (2006) *Critical Lessons: What Our Schools Should Teach*. Cambridge: Cambridge University Press.

Norman, K (ed) (1992) *Thinking Voices: The Work of the National Oracy Project*. London: Hodder & Stoughton.

Nystrand, M, Wu, L, Gamoran, A, Zeisler, S and Long, D (2003) Questions in Time: Investigating the Structure and Dynamics of Unfolding Classroom Discourse. *Discourse Processes*, 35(2): 135–98.

O'Connor, C, Michaels, S and Chapin, S (2015) 'Scaling Down' to Explore the Role of Talk in Learning: From District Intervention to Controlled Classroom Study. In Resnick, L, Asterhan, C and Clarke, S (eds) *Socializing Intelligence Through Academic Talk and Dialogue* (pp 111–26). Washington, DC: AERA.

O'Connor, C, Michaels, S, Chapin, S and Harbaugh, A (2017) The Silent and the Vocal: Participation and Learning in Whole-class Discussion. *Learning and Instruction*, 48: 5–13.

Organization for Economic Cooperation and Development (OECD) (2005) *The Definition and Selection of Key Competencies*. [online] Available at: www.oecd.org/pisa/35070367.pdf (accessed 30 June 2019).

Organization for Economic Cooperation and Development (OECD) (2018) *The Future of Education and Skills: Education 2030*. [online] Available at: www.oecd.org/education/2030/E2030%20Position%20Paper%20(05.04.2018).pdf (accessed 30 June 2019).

Oliver, M and Venville, G (2015) Cognitive Acceleration Through Science Education: The CASE for Thinking Through Science. In Wegerif, R, Li, L and Kaufman, J (eds) *The Routledge International Handbook of Research on Teaching Thinking*. Abingdon: Routledge.

Oxford University Press (2018) *Why Closing the Word Gap Matters: Oxford Language Report.* [online] Available at: http://fdslive.oup.com/www.oup.com/oxed/Oxford-Language-Report.PDF?region=uk (accessed 30 June 2019).

Palinscar, A and Brown, A (1984) Reciprocal Teaching of Comprehension-fostering and Comprehension-monitoring Activities. *Cognition and Instruction*, 1(2): 117–75.

Pauli, C and Reusser, K (2015) Discursive Cultures of Learning in (Everyday) Mathematics Teaching: A Video-based Study on Mathematics Teaching in German and Swiss Classrooms. In Resnick, L, Asterhan, C and Clarke, S (eds) *Socializing Intelligence Through Academic Talk and Dialogue* (pp 181–93). Washington: AERA.

Perry, J, Lundie, D and Golder, G (2018) Metacognition in Schools: What Does the Literature Suggest About the Effectiveness of Teaching Metacognition in Schools? *Educational Review.* DOI: 10.1080/00131911.2018.1441127.

Philpott, C and Poultney, V (2018) *Evidence-based Teaching: A Critical Overview for Enquiring Teachers.* St Albans: Critical Publishing.

Piaget, J (1950) *The Psychology of Intelligence.* Abingdon: Routledge.

Piaget, J (1977) *The Development of Thought.* New York: Viking.

Pierce, K and Gilles, C (2008) From Exploratory Talk to Critical Conversations in Mercer, N and Hodkinson, S (eds) *Exploring Talk in School* (pp 37–53). London: Sage.

Pino-Pasternak, D, Whitebread, D and Neale, D (2018) The Role of Regulatory, Social, and Dialogic Dynamics on Young Children's Productive Collaboration in Group Problem Solving. *New Directions for Child and Adolescent Development*, 162: 41–66.

Rajala, A, Hilppo, J and Lipponen, L (2012) The Emergence of Inclusive Exploratory Talk in Primary Students' Peer Interaction. *International Journal of Educational Research*, 53: 55–67.

Resnick, L and Schantz, F (2015) Talking to Learn: The Promise and Challenge of Dialogic Teaching. In Resnick, L, Asterhan, C and Clarke, S (eds) *Socializing Intelligence Through Academic Talk and Dialogue* (pp 441–50). Washington, DC: AERA.

Reznitskaya, A, Glina, M, Carolan, B, Michaud, O, Rogers, J and Sequeira, L (2012) Examining Transfer Effects from Dialogic Discussions to New Tasks and Contexts. *Contemporary Educational Psychology*, 37(4): 288–306.

Reznitskaya, A and Gregory, M (2013) Student Thought and Classroom Language: Examining the Mechanisms of Change in Dialogic Teaching. *Educational Psychologist*, 48(2): 114–33.

Reznitskaya, A, Kuo, L, Clark, A, Miller, B, Jadallah, M, Anderson, R and Nguyen-Jahiel, K (2009) Collaborative Reasoning: A Dialogic Approach to Group Discussions. *Cambridge Journal of Education*, 39(1): 29–48.

Ritchhart, R (2015) *Creating Cultures of Thinking: The 8 Forces We Must Master to Truly Transform Our Schools*. San Francisco: Jossey-Bass.

Rogoff, B (1990) *Apprenticeship in Thinking: Cognitive Development in Social Context*. Oxford: Oxford University Press.

Rojas-Drummond, S and Mercer, N (2003) Scaffolding the Development of Effective Collaboration and Learning. *International Journal of Educational Research*, 39(1–2): 99–111.

Rojas-Drummond, S, Mazon, N, Littleton, K and Velez, M (2014) Developing Reading Comprehension Through Collaborative Learning. *Journal of Research in Reading*, 37(2): 138–58.

Rowe, M (1978) *Teaching Science as Continuous Inquiry*. New York: McGraw-Hill.

Sahlberg, P (2016) Finnish Schools and the Global Education Reform Movement. In Evers, J and Kneyber, R (ed) *Flip the System: Changing Education from the Ground Up* (pp 162–74). Abingdon: Routledge.

Schmitz, M and Winskel, H (2008) Towards Effective Partnerships in a Collaborative Problem-solving Task. *British Journal of Educational Psychology*, 78: 581–96.

Scott, P (2008) Talking a Way to Understanding in Science Classrooms. In Mercer, N and Hodkinson, S (eds) *Exploring Talk in School* (pp 17–36). London: Sage.

Scott, P and Mortimer, E (2006) The Tension Between Authoritative and Dialogic Discourse: A Fundamental Characteristic of Meaning Making Interactions in High School Science Lessons. *Science Education*, 90(4): 605–31.

Sedova, K, Salamounova, Z and Svaricek, R (2014) Troubles With Dialogic Teaching. *Learning Culture and Social Interaction*, 3: 274–85.

Shayer, M (1999) Cognitive Acceleration Through Science Education II: Its Effects and Scope. *International Journal of Science Education*, 21(8): 883–902.

Sinclair, J and Coulthard, R (1975) *Towards an Analysis of Discourse: The English Used by Teachers and Pupils*. Oxford: Oxford University Press.

Skidmore, D (2006) Pedagogy and Dialogue. *Cambridge Journal of Education*, 36(4): 503–14.

Skidmore, D and Murakami, K (2012) Claiming Our Own Space: Polyphony in Teacher–Student Dialogue. *Linguistics and Education*, 23: 200–10.

Smith, F, Hardman, F, Wall, K and Mroz, M (2004) Interactive Whole Class Teaching in the National Literacy and Numeracy Strategies. *British Educational Research Journal*, 30(3): 395–411.

Snell, J and Lefstein, A (2018) 'Low Ability', Participation and Identity in Dialogic Pedagogy. *American Educational Research Journal*, 55(1): 40–78.

Snowling, M, Hulme, C, Bailey, A, Stothard, S and Lindsay, G (2011) *Better Communication Research Programme: Language and Literacy Attainment of Pupils During Early Years and Through KS2: Does Teacher Assessment at Five Provide a Valid Measure Of Children's Current and Future Educational Attainments?* DfE Research Brief 172a. [online] Available at: https://files.eric. ed.gov/fulltext/ED526910.pdf (accessed 30 June 2019).

Sun, J, Anderson, R, Lin, T and Morris, J (2015) Social and Cognitive Development During Collaborative Reasoning. In Resnick, L, Asterhan, C and Clarke, S (eds) *Socializing Intelligence Through Academic Talk and Dialogue* (pp 63–75). Washington, DC: AERA.

Sutton Trust (2012) *Social Mobility and Education Gaps in the Four Major Anglophone Countries: Research Findings for the Social Mobility Summit.* [online] Available at: www.suttontrust.com/research-paper/social-mobility-report-2012-summit (accessed 30 June 2019).

Sweller, J (2016) Working Memory, Long-Term Memory and Instructional Design. *Journal of Applied Research in Memory and Cognition*, 5: 360–67.

Tan, C (2017) The Enactment of the Policy Initiative for Critical Thinking in Singapore Schools. *Journal of Education Policy*, 32(5): 588–603.

Topping, K and Trickey, S (2007) Collaborative Philosophical Inquiry for Schoolchildren: Cognitive Gains at a 2-Year Follow-Up. *British Journal of Educational Psychology*, 77: 787–96.

Topping, K and Trickey, S (2014) The Role of Dialog in Philosophy for Children. *International Journal of Educational Research*, 63: 69–78.

Townsend, A (2013) *Action Research: The Challenges of Understanding and Researching Practice.* Maidenhead: McGraw-Hill.

Trickey, S and Topping, K (2004) 'Philosophy for Children': A Systematic Review. *Research Papers in Education*, 19(3): 365–80.

Tytler, R and Aranda, G (2015) Expert Teachers' Discursive Moves in Science Classroom Interactive Talk. *International Journal of Science and Mathematics Education*, 13: 425–46.

Vaish, V (2008) Interactional Patterns in Singapore's English Classrooms. *Linguistics and Education*, 19(4): 366–77.

Van de Pol, J, Volman, M and Beishuizen, J (2010) Scaffolding in Teacher–Student Interaction: A Decade of Research. *Educational Psychology Review*, 22: 271–96.

Van der Veen, C, de Mey, L, van Kruistum, C and van Oers, B (2017) The Effect of Classroom Talk and Metacommunication on Young Children's Oral Communicative Competence and Subject Matter Knowledge: An Intervention Study in Early Childhood Education. *Learning and Instruction*, 48: 14–22.

Vass, E, Littleton, K, Jones, A and Miell, D (2014) The Affectively Constituted Dimensions of Creative Interthinking. *International Journal of Educational Research*, 66: 63–77.

Visible Learning Plus (2018) *250+ Influences on Student Achievement.* [online] Available at: https://us.corwin.com/sites/default/files/250_influences_10.1.2018.pdf (accessed 30 June 2019).

Vrikki, M, Wheatley, L, Howe, C, Hennessy, S and Mercer, N (2019) Dialogic Practices in Primary School Classrooms. *Language and Education*, 33(1): 85–100.

Vygotsky, L (1978) *Mind in Society: The Development of Higher Psychological Processes.* Cambridge, MA: Harvard University Press.

Vygotsky, L (1986) *Thought and Language.* Cambridge, MA: MIT Press.

Wangru, C (2016) On Teacher Talk From the Perspective of Dialogue Theory. *Cross Cultural Communication*, 12(5): 38–46.

Watkins, C (2005) Classrooms as Learning Communities: A Review of Research. *London Review of Education*, 3(1): 47–64.

Webb, N, Franke, M, Ing, M, Wong, J, Fernandez, C, Shin, N and Turrou, A (2014) Engaging With Others' Mathematical Idea: Interrelationships Among Student Participation, Teachers' Instructional Practices and Learning. *International Journal of Educational Research*, 63: 79–93.

Webb, P, Whitlow, J and Venter, D (2017) From Exploratory Talk to Abstract Reasoning: A Case for Far Transfer? *Educational Psychology Review*, 29: 565–81.

Wegerif, R (2007) *Dialogic Teaching and Technology.* New York: Springer.

Wegerif, R (2011) Towards a Dialogic Theory of How Children Think and Learn. *Thinking Skills and Creativity*, 6: 179–90.

Wegerif, R and Dawes, L (2004) *Thinking and Learning with ICT: Raising Achievement in Primary Classrooms*. Abingdon: Routledge.

Wells, G (1999) *Dialogic Inquiry: Toward a Sociocultural Practice and Theory of Education*. Cambridge: Cambridge University Press.

Wells, G and Arauz, R (2006) Dialogue in the Classroom. *The Journal of the Learning Sciences*, 15(3): 379–428.

Wertsch, J (1991) *Voices of the Mind*. Cambridge: Harvard University Press.

Wertsch, J (2008) From Social Interaction to Higher Psychological Processes: A Clarification and Application of Vygotsky's Theory. *Human Development*, 51: 66–79.

Wiliam, D (2006) Assessment for Learning: Why, What and How. In *Cambridge Assessment Network Excellence in Assessment: Assessment for Learning, a Supplement to the Cambridge Assessment Network Assessment for Learning Seminar held on 15 September 2006 in Cambridge UK*. [online] Available at: www.assessnet.org.uk/e-learning/file.php/1/Resources/Excellence_in_Assessment/Excellence_in_Assessment_-_Issue_1.pdf (accessed 30 June 2019).

Wiliam, D (2013) *Engineering Effective Tasks, Activities and Discussions That Elicit Evidence of Learning*. [online] Available at: www.dylanwiliam.org (accessed 30 June 2019).

Wiliam, D (2017) *Getting Educational Research Right*. [online] Available at: https://medium.com/@thersa/getting-educational-research-right-b77fbc82ef6e (accessed 30 June 2019).

Wilkinson, A (1965) The Concept of Oracy. *English in Education*, 2(A2): 3–5.

Wilkinson, A (1970) The Concept of Oracy. *The English Journal*, 59: 71–7.

Willingham, D (2007) Critical Thinking: Why Is It So Hard To Teach? *American Educator*, Summer 2007: 8–19.

Wood, D, Bruner, J and Ross, G (1976) The Role of Tutoring in Problem Solving. *Journal of Child Psychiatry*, 17: 89–100.

Wrigley, T (2018) The Power of 'Evidence': Reliable Science or a Set of Blunt Tools? *British Educational Research Journal*, 44 (3): 359–76.

Wubbels, T (2007) Do We Know a Community of Practice When We See One? *Technology, Pedagogy and Education*, 16(2): 225–33.

Young, M (2013) Overcoming the Crisis in Curriculum Theory: A Knowledge-based Approach. *Journal of Curriculum Studies*, 45: 101–18.

Zepeda, C, Hlutkowsky, C, Partika, A and Nokes-Malach, T (2018) Identifying Teachers' Supports of Metacognition Through Classroom Talk and Its Relation To Growth in Conceptual Learning. *Journal of Educational Psychology*. Advance online publication. [online] Available at: http://dx.doi.org/10.1037/edu0000300 (accessed 30 June 2019).

Zimmerman, B (2002) Becoming a Self-regulated Learner: An Overview. *Theory into Practice*, 41(2): 64–70.

Index

Printed in the United States
by Baker & Taylor Publisher Services